Excellence in the Boardroom

"Bill Dimma, with his forty years experience of directorship, has explored the most pressing governance issues in today's complex business environment in an invaluable resource book. This is a must-read for current and future directors."
— *Jack L. Cockwell, Co-Chairman, Brascan Corporation*

"Written by an experienced practitioner and long-term advocate of good corporate governance, Bill Dimma's *Excellence in the Boardroom* is a practical, sensible, pragmatic collection of observations and comments on the many facets of this important topic."
— *Lynton Wilson, Chairman of the Board,*
Nortel Networks Corporation

"*Excellence in the Boardroom* presents the insider's view on successful corporate directorship. In combining extensive coverage on key issues in board governance with insightful, first-hand reflections, Bill Dimma gives us powerful knowledge with practical sense."
— *C.Douglas Caldwell, Chairman, The Caldwell Partners*

"As a fellow director, I have observed Bill Dimma's knowledge of, and dedication to, the art of corporate governance. He has created a wonderful, comprehensive reference book based on a lifetime of experience."
— *Richard F. Haskayne, Chairman,*
TransCanada Pipelines and Fording Inc.

EXCELLENCE
IN THE
BOARDROOM

EXCELLENCE
IN THE
BOARDROOM

BEST PRACTICES IN
CORPORATE DIRECTORSHIP

WILLIAM A. DIMMA

John Wiley & Sons Canada Ltd
22 Worcester Road
Etobicoke, Ontario
M9W 1L1

National Library of Canada Cataloguing in Publication Data

Dimma, William A. (William Andrew), 1928-
    Excellence in the boardroom : best practices in corporate directorship

Includes index.
ISBN 0-470-83160-X

    1. Boards of directors. 2. Corporate governance. I. Title.

HD2741.D54 2002   658.4'22   C2002-900286-9

Production Credits
Text and Cover Design: Interrobang Graphic Design Inc.
Printer: Tri-Graphic Printing

Printed in Canada
10 9 8 7 6 5 4 3 2 1

A merchant was there, on a high-saddled horse...
So impressive and dignified his bearing
As he went about his loans and bargaining.
He was a really estimable man,
But the fact is I never learnt his name.

> — From the *General Dialogue*,
>   *The Canterbury Tales*, Geoffrey Chaucer

There he goes busily about his business,
Buying and borrowing but never dicing,
And never dancing, but in short behaving just like
a businessman—
so there I'll leave him.

> — From *The Sea Captain's Tale*,
>   *The Canterbury Tales*, Geoffrey Chaucer

Contents

Foreword   xiii

Acknowledgements   xviii

INTRODUCTION   1

PART 1: ON THE BOARD: DEFINING A VISION   9

CHAPTER 1: THE PERFECT BOARD   11
The Ideal Structure   12
The Ideal Processes   14
Summary   20

CHAPTER 2: BOARD MANNERS AND THE
      DIRECTOR FROM HELL   23

CHAPTER 3: THINGS BOARDS COULD DO BETTER   27
1.   Adopt a Sensitive, Individual Director
     Assessment Program   27

2. Forego Compulsory Retirement for Directors   28
3. Simplify Governance for Smaller Companies   29
4. Expect All Directors to Stay Current Through
   Ongoing Education and Training   30
5. Delegate CEO Succession Issues to Boards,
   Even With 100%-Owned Subsidiaries   30
6. Delegate the Selection of New Directors to
   Board Chairman and/or a Board Committee,
   Even With 100%-Owned Subsidiaries   31
7. Use Performance Options More Frequently
   and Routinely   32
8. Separate the Roles of Board Chairman and CEO,
   Except in Unusual Circumstances   33
9. As Directors, Speak Out Frankly and Fearlessly,
   Though Civilly, When Necessary   34
10. As Directors, Avoid Potential, Let Alone Actual,
    Conflicts of Interests   35

CHAPTER 4: TEN BEST PRACTICES OF MODERN
CORPORATE GOVERNANCE   37

SOME PERSONAL EXPERIENCES AS A DIRECTOR (I)   43

PART 2: GETTING IN GEAR: HOW TO MAKE IT WORK   49

CHAPTER 5: BOARD AND DIRECTOR EVALUATION   51

CHAPTER 6: ADVISORY BOARDS   57
More On Advisory Boards   60

CHAPTER 7: BOARD RESPONSIBILITIES   69
Board Chairman and CEO Roles: Separation or Not?   69

CEO Succession Planning 74
    Wholly Owned Companies 74
    Legally Constituted Board 75
    Controlling Shareholder 77
    From Experience 78
    Widely Held Corporation 80
    Ideal Scenario 81
Director Retirement 84
The Board of Directors and Pension Fund
    Management 86

SOME PERSONAL EXPERIENCES AS A DIRECTOR (II) 95

PART 3: THE FINE PRINT:
    COMPENSATION AND ACCREDITATION 101

Chapter 8: Compensation of Company Directors 103

Chapter 9: Director Accreditation 117

Chapter 10: Executive Compensation Issues 123
Stock Options for Executives 134
Some Current Issues with Stock Options 138
Executive Pensions 145

Some Personal Experiences as a Director (III) 155

PART 4: THE RUBBER MEETS THE ROAD:
    CHALLENGES FACING CORPORATIONS 161

CHAPTER 11: CORPORATE RESPONSIBILITY 163
More On Shareholder vs Stakeholder Capitalism 170

CHAPTER 12: INSTITUTIONAL INVESTORS   175

**CHAPTER 13: SOME CONTEMPORARY BOARD ISSUES:
    HOSTILE TAKEOVERS**   187
Some Differences Between U.S. and Canadian
    Corporate Boards   191
Liabilities Where Due Diligence is No Defense   194
Postscript   197

SOME PERSONAL EXPERIENCES AS A DIRECTOR (IV)   199

**CHAPTER 14: THREE CORE PRINCIPLES OF EFFECTIVE
    COPORATE GOVERNANCE**   205

**APPENDIX A: PUBLIC COMPANY DIRECTOR
    ACCREDITATION**   215

**APPENDIX B: PAST AND CURRENT BOARDS OF THE
    AUTHOR (1963 TO 2002)**   229

INDEX   233

Foreword

All too often, we hear about how dramatically the role of directors has changed in recent years. That, unlike the past, the impact of technology and global business dynamics now place directors in high-pressure and difficult positions. While the context may have changed, the duties and responsibilities of directors have not.

What has changed and made this situation different is that, in the wake of major corporate fiascoes, boards have been placed in the fishbowl of public scrutiny. Interestingly enough, after the requisite post-mortems were done and the ensuing noise from corporate governance pundits dissipated, it became quite clear that the cause for such debacles was simply that these boards had lost sight of the fundamentals of governing business corporations. Quite simply, they had dropped the ball in questioning management on such "complex issues" as the integrity of earnings, projections and timely disclosure of vital information to shareholders. Had these directors taken the time to remember the fundamentals of sound business judgment and exercised the old duty of care, shareholders and the capital markets in general would have been better and more responsibly served. Instead, we heard claims of temporary governance insanity driven by analyst expectations, daily stock prices and other pressures invoked in the name of "sustainable, long-term shareholder value."

Against this apparent breakdown of governance principles, Corporate Canada finds itself in the unusual situation where a generation of corporate directors is retiring from many boards and their successors are being ushered into our boardrooms bringing a combination of business acumen, a sincere interest to serve, mixed with a healthy dose of apprehension of finding themselves in the fishbowl without the benefit of swimming lessons.

Where does this new generation learn how to be corporate directors and deal effectively with the issues brought to their boards? Where do they learn about good and bad board decisions when there is no institutional memory to rely on?

That is why Bill Dimma's book is such a valuable contribution to corporate governance in Canada. It combines the pragmatism of a savvy businessman with the vast knowledge and experience of a veteran of more than 80 boards, who, over four decades of board service, has not been afraid of confronting issues, no matter how difficult or sensitive. This book is important because it offers views and opinions about what works and doesn't work in real life board situations. From that standpoint, this book is also courageous and refreshing.

Among other things, this book is also short in theory and long in practice. It is grounded in reality and written with the dedication and passion of someone who considers his service on boards both a privilege and a duty. A duty to various constituencies, including those who are following him into the boardrooms of Canadian companies and with whom he feels he must share his experience. In doing so, Bill demonstrates not just a sense of caring, but also the understanding that the new directors will need to be armed with as much knowledge and information as possible if they are to navigate these board waters successfully.

This book is about experiences and learning. It provides practical advice on how to deal with the governance dilemmas facing corporate directors today in an arena where the boundaries shift constantly. Bill's sound advice gives directors the tools that allow them to effectively combine independent thinking with meaningful contributions to the collective.

The corporate fiascoes of the last few years have been invariably followed by strident calls for reform and the predictable appointment of Commissions and Task Forces, which prescribed the need to change board processes, structures and responsibilities as remedies for this corporate malaise.

I suggest that, instead of going down the traditional road of complex and impossible to implement reforms, we provide boards with copies of Bill Dimma's book as a reminder that good judgment, courage, ethical principles and accountability to shareholders need not be restructured nor reinvented because, deep down, directors want to do what is right for companies and their shareholders. This book will help them do just that with the benefit of Bill's personal insights gathered in almost one hundred companies in more than 30 different industries and many non-profit organizations. In trying to quantify the value of this book to directors, I am reminded of a quote from G.K. Chesterton: "It isn't that they can't see the solution. It is that they can't see the problem."

Those who assume that Bill's advice is of the legal or regulatory variety will be pleased to discover that it is not. Readers will find neither suggestions nor encouragement to reach for legal oracles to support directors' actions and behaviours.

This is a courageous book because it successfully counters the scepticism of an intended audience that, after the corporate governance barrage of recent years, has literally overdosed on prescriptions that somehow have failed to keep the patient out of intensive care.

What is different about this book is that it makes available to the reader the accumulated experience of the author in the art of corporate governance but presented in a no-nonsense, down-to-earth, highly practical way for directors to effectively assess and successfully resolve most of the problems encountered in boardrooms.

This book will be a very useful and practical guide to those currently serving as board directors. The boardroom equivalent of a night-table consultation and reflection book. To those who aspire to be directors, it will be a worthwhile source of knowledge and a valuable how-to manual. In fact, I would recommend that boards adopt readings from this book as regular agenda items to monitor the governance practices of their boards.

Bill's career as a director stands on its record and needs no promotion from anyone. It has been characterized by true professionalism grounded in ethical principles, values and always doing what he knows to be right. That so many companies and non-profit organizations have sought him out to serve on their boards is testimony of Bill's sound judgement, perception, independent thinking and his realistic view of the world of business. Over these four decades, Bill has helped create, shape and improve many of the unwritten governance standards that Canadian boards live by today.

By providing advice and guidance to two generations of directors, Bill Dimma has performed an extraordinary service to Canadian business and to the fellowship of corporate directors.

Marcelo D. Mackinlay
Chairman
Institute of Corporate Directors

Acknowledgements

I want to express my deep gratitude to Gordon Hall, Vice Chairman of William M. Mercer Limited until his retirement at the end of 2001, and to Marcelo Mackinlay, Chairman of the Institute of Corporate Directors, for their steady and unflagging support for this book. Their help has been a source of much comfort to me. Without it, this book would have come to press later at best and perhaps not at all. That can and should be said also about the consistently friendly and professional advice (and diplomatic reminders of deadlines) provided by Karen Milner, Executive Editor, and Elizabeth McCurdy, Associate Editor, at the Canadian offices of John Wiley and Sons.

Introduction

This book is an adaptation and enlargement of some three dozen articles written for *Director*, the house organ of the Institute of Corporate Directors, published between 1995 and 2001.

Why did I (and others) think it worthwhile to convert a miscellany of thoughts on a wide range of board-related topics into what I hope is a coherent look at directorship, which is and will remain more art than science?

As background, let me say at the outset that I have sat on fifty corporate and another forty not-for-profit boards, beginning in 1963. I mention this neither to impress nor to evoke sympathy, but rather to make the point that this book is primarily based on experience. I like to think that it is not inconsistent with sound theory but, in the inevitable mix of practice and theory, I have bowed to practice first, theory second. Or to recall a one-liner cited by Jim Nininger, then president of the Conference Board of Canada, at a Bilderberg meeting that we both once attended, "That may work in practice but it will never work in theory."

Now to why it has seemed worthwhile to produce this slim volume about the world of business from a board-room perspective. Over the years, I have been increasingly convinced that good governance matters, though I am well aware that, somewhat surprisingly, this view is not held universally. I believe that good governance leads to, and is one of the principal causes of good corporate performance.

Sadly, the correlation is neither perfect nor measurable. Many macro-level factors, both malignant and benign, are usually at work. A few of the more obvious ones include the state of the economy, the level of stock markets, interest rates, inflation, and the ideological bent of government.

And then there are a host of industry and enterprise-specific variables: unpredictable, idiosyncratic, often crucial. They can affect any given enterprise at some point. These can, of course, have an enormous influence, positive or negative, for richer or poorer, on corporate fortunes. One of these variables is the quality of management. Here, however, there is almost always an effect-and-cause correlation with the quality of governance, especially when boards appoint management instead of the reverse.

Being in the right business at the right time is not only a matter of sound strategy, though it helps. There is also an element of luck involved. And even those of us who subscribe generally to the maxim that we make our own luck will concede that it ain't necessarily so.

Disclaimers aside, let me reassert vigourously that good governance matters. It matters a great deal more than the many sceptics and cynics are willing to admit. There is no shortage of doubting Thomases who, in responding to that well-worn question, "Where were the directors?" focus on the exceptions and not on what is more common and usual. The criticism levied against the fairly few companies where things go badly and sometimes fatally wrong overshadows the kudos due to the many companies where, for the most part, things go right. As a result, many observers are persuaded to give credence to a distorted and jaundiced view of corporate reality. If good governance matters—and, to repeat, I believe fervently that it does—a book which tries to describe some of the causes and components of good governance is worth writing. It is also, I hope, worth reading.

It would, of course, be the height of hubris to pretend to have all or even most of the answers, but I am not so humble as to disavow having any. I have always espoused the generalization that experience is a superior teacher. Without experience, one is flying blind. And, as someone once said, "To the blind, all things are sudden." And negative experiences, of which I've had my share, are usually better teachers than positive ones. Certainly we remember them longer.

Any experienced director who sits or has sat on several boards, and who tells you that he hasn't seen an occasional example of greed, stupidity, insensitivity, abdication, massive ego, bad judgement, and short-sightedness, is in denial or at least unwilling to discuss frankly these all-too-human flaws and frailties. And these are only seven of the many more than seven deadly sins of the corporate world and, for that matter, all worlds where people come together for a purpose.

In 1963, I joined my first board. An old friend and his wife incorporated a retail business in Toronto. They named it the Florentine Shop. The board was made up of the two of them and me, the legal minimum size for a corporate entity. During the three or four years that I was a director of that company, we met in person only once or twice. I was always aware that my principal, if not only, role was to provide the requisite third body and a rather inconsequential one at that, since share ownership resided entirely with the other two bodies.

In essence, a friend asked me to do him a little favour—what the Creoles in Louisiana call a lagniappe—and I was pleased to oblige. The term *corporate governance* had not yet been uttered nor the concept invented. Even if it had been, my contribution in terms of governance would, I fear, have been roughly in proportion to my directorial experience at the time.

That was thirty-nine years ago. How far we have travelled since then. Books about boards and directors with hesitant titles, like *Directors: Myth and Reality* (Myles Mace) or *Pawns and Potentates* (Jay Lorsch), or sharply questioning titles like *Who's in Charge Here, Anyway?* (Adam Zimmerman), were succeeded by those with more self-confident titles, like *The New Corporate Directors* (Charles Anderson and Robert Anthony) or *Making Boards Work* (David Leighton and Don Thain).

We have in fact come so far that, as in so many endeavours where change arrives rather suddenly and subsequent progress is at first rapid, an inevitable reaction sits in. So, today, we hear plaintive comments like these:

- Enough! Let's pause to regroup. Governance today focuses too much on process at the expense of results.

- Let's digest what we've done over the past decade or so before we embark on still another new round of governance initiatives.

- Too many pundits, academics, theorists, and perpetual "anti-establishment" voices are clamouring to influence the corporate governance agenda. They lack practical experience and a sufficient understanding of what it takes to oversee and run a successful enterprise in today's uber-competitive world.

I recognize that some of these comments stem from legitimate concerns and fears. They lead me to state clearly and simply three overarching premises which support the thrust of this book. These are:

1. A board can't manage and management shouldn't and mustn't govern. Boards govern, provide oversight, ensure that there is first-class management and that there is orderly succession. Management organizes and executes. Together, they develop a vision for the longer-term and a strategy for the mid-term (any strategy in today's environment with longer than a three-year time horizon should be viewed quizzically). All of this is elementary, well known, and widely accepted.

In the same vein, management reports to a board and a chairman, who report in turn to shareholders. Or one can say, with only a slight variation in meaning, that the CEO, as senior management representative, reports to shareholders through a chairman and a board. This begs the question of separation or not of the roles of chairman and CEO, a topic discussed more than once in this book.

2. The relationship between a board and management in general and, even more importantly, between a board chairman and a CEO in particular, is crucial. As I argue later in the text, this relationship cannot, must not, be blatantly and chronically adversarial. But neither, can it be like "home on the range... where never is heard a discouraging word."

Creative tension is the best phrase I've been able to find over the years to describe the ideal relationship between a chairman and a CEO. I use this phrase frequently in this book. This assumes, of course, that one person with two roles isn't talking to himself or, less infrequently these days, herself.[1]

The term *creative tension*[2] implies a culture and a relationship of mutual trust and respect between two individuals who understand that there are two separate and distinct roles to play. In those situations where there is ample potential for disagreement, such as executive compensation, entrenchment of management rights, and CEO succession, matters are

---

[1] Whenever words like "he" or "him" or "his" or "himself" are used throughout this text, they are intended to include "she," or "her" or "herself." The English language does not accomodate, except awkwardly, gender-free usage in the singular case.

[2] An alternative term is constructive interaction.

resolved civilly and maturely. I recognize that, only in the best of all possible worlds, is this as easily done as said.

3. Finally, governance must not subordinate results to process. I am well aware that this sounds dangerously like saying that the end justifies the means. That's not what I intend but rather that, subject to legal, regulatory, ethical, and human constraints and considerations, process must never dominate and take precedence over results, however measured. On the choice of measurements, it is always instructive to remember that shareholders must be the final beneficiaries.

I should emphasize that these three generalizations are most applicable to widely held companies without a controlling shareholder. In certain respects, they apply less to companies with a controlling shareholder or group along with minority shareholders. They apply still less to private companies owned either by another company (in which case they're wholly owned subsidiaries) or by a small control group, whether corporations or individuals. Depending on which of these broad classes of company is involved, areas like management succession, executive compensation, and the separation of roles of chairman and CEO are handled differently, both in practice and prescriptively.

I should like to caution the reader that this book contains nothing revolutionary. No call to the ramparts is issued here. The blare of trumpets shall not be heard. I do not advocate massive change from the status quo, but rather continuing fine-tuning. Those who favour, at one extreme, the elimination of boards altogether on the grounds that they do not make a difference or, at the other extreme, the reduction of management to little more than a subservient executor of the orders of an autocratic board will find no solace here.

I subscribe to the conventional generalization that the board and management are there to serve the shareholder, first and foremost. This is clearly required *de jure* and is also an accurate description *de facto*. I support it prescriptively as well. This is not, of course, to argue that the best interests of other stakeholders ought not to be considered carefully and seriously. And sometimes such interests should be acceded to, consistent with the best long-run interests of shareholders.

But in a free market society, I find the argument that one or more of a wide range of stakeholders are, in effect, co-owners of an enterprise—and I exaggerate only slightly the claims made by some—to be not only impractical but dysfunctional. The interests of shareholders are and must remain paramount, although the time frame for serving these interests will vary from company to company, from decision to decision, and from crest to trough in the economic cycle.

This prologue should now be ended, before it is subsumed into a book in its own right. If I stray in the main text from the few principles I've enunciated here, *mea culpa*. I hope that each of you who ventures into what follows may find one or more insights that will add a lumen or two to the still insufficiently lit boardroom.

PART 1

On Board:
Defining a Vision

CHAPTER 1

The
Perfect Board

I have often thought about the perfect board: its structure, its processes, its interactions. I suppose what I mean is the ideal board—the best of what's out there—since perfection exists only in a few gems and supermodels and much of Mozart.

But some boards are clearly superior to others and while perfection (or even best of breed) is, like beauty, in the eye of the beholder or perhaps the shareholder, some useful generalizations can be drawn. Of course, to some degree, boards must be tailored to their circumstances and their environment.

THE IDEAL STRUCTURE

1. The Chairman[1] and the CEO are two different persons. While some highly successful companies don't follow this advice, the separation of functions is, in governance terms, almost invariably preferable. Furthermore, the chairman is not the retired former CEO.

2. The board has seven to twelve members, give or take a director or two. If larger, speech-making replaces discussion. If smaller, the diversity of views and experience is too limited.

3. No more than two members of management sit on the board of their company. The CEO is a member but the presence of the CFO or even the COO is more debatable. What is gained in helping a COO, perhaps an heir apparent, to acquire boardroom exposure and experience and what is gained by having an extra knowledge base at the table are offset by two negatives. Board members who report to the CEO are unlikely to be either vocal or frank in their comments. Furthermore, the CEO may himself be less open and candid when his direct reports are present.

4. There is a full range of board committees, at least four in larger companies. The names and function will vary somewhat from company to company. Commonly, there are audit, compensation and human resource, governance, and nominating committees. Investment, public affairs, and environment committees tend to be more common only in certain industries. Members of

---

[1] Another term used generically to include both genders.

management are not committee members. They attend either without a vote or at the call of the chair.

5. Board committees are small. Three or, at most, four directors are ample. If an objective is to ensure that every director sits on at least one committee, the solution is to reduce the size of the board, not to increase the size of committees.

6. Especially with smaller boards, there is insufficient justification for an executive committee; it introduces a divisive caste system into a board's culture. Should some specialized need for an executive committee exist, such as consistently frequent board-level decisions, which can't wait until the next regular meeting, optimum membership is the board chair, all committee chairs, and the CEO, ex officio. It meets only when absolutely necessary.

7. On board composition, directors are selected and appointed to serve the specific needs of a given company. While this seems obvious, it is surprising how often it is insufficiently taken into account. Choose some but not all persons who know your industry and some but not all persons who reside near your head office or your principal markets.

   Political correctness for its own sake is not yielded to. But, given the diversity of accomplished people out there, boards should be somewhat more heterogeneous than they are.

   Wherever possible, avoid constituency boards in which at least one director owes a duty of allegiance and loyalty to some external constituency, such as a labour union or other special-interest group. Their potential for divisiveness is almost always greater than any latent capacity for drawing a constituency into the tent.

The vast majority of shareholder-owned companies are not required to include constituency directors on their boards. On the other hand, many not-for-profit organizations do have such a requirement. For example, almost all university and hospital boards are required to include constituency directors.

Fortunately, this is not much of an issue for not-for-profits, which tend to represent and serve multi-contituencies. For-profits, on the other hand, serve corporate and shareholder interests primarily if not solely, certainly *de jure* and, largely, *de facto*.

THE IDEAL PROCESSES

1. The chairman leads the board and plays a central role in relationships with shareholders. The CEO leads the company and management. This definitely does not mean two solitudes. Rather there is an almost seamless continuum of two highly interactive components of a coherent organization.

2. The board chairman and the CEO are not buddies nor, except rarely, are they old friends. Neither are they rivals or antagonists. There is a mutual respect between them, both on a personal level and for each other's role. But there is also that creative tension, which recognizes that, on some issues, there will be overlapping responsibilities for problems and issues which must be resolved maturely.

The CEO truly believes and accepts that the board is the agent of the shareholder and that he answers to the shareholder through the board and its chairman.

The chairman truly believes and accepts that there is a profound difference between governing and managing. He and his board respect the boundary, which is sufficiently ill-defined that both good judgement and goodwill are needed.

Both board and management understand the Scylla and Charybdis of abdication on the one hand and undue interference or micro-management on the other.

3. The board is involved centrally and intensively at various stages in the process of strategy formulation, evaluation, and regular updating and revision.

Assuming the company revisits its strategic plan annually, the board is involved early when ideas are sought and evaluated, at mid-point when the outline of the plan has been adumbrated but change is still possible, and late in the process when the plan is essentially complete. At this point, the board's role is to buy in, perhaps with some footnoted observations or reservations, and to put its formal imprimatur on the plan.

The strategic plan looks ahead about three years. Once, when the world was young, companies used to make five-year, ten-year and even, occasionally, longer plans. As an engineer less than ten years out of university, I worked on the economic justification of a very large ethylene plant which had a seventeen-year payback and a twenty-year horizon. But today's world is too unpredictable, uncertain, even capricious, too marked by discontinuity and volatility. Even a five-year plan requires more hubris and less humility than most CEOs—though not usually perceived as shrinking violets—possess.

A sophisticated board does not confuse or commingle annual budgeting or business plans with strategic plans or strategic thinking. Furthermore, neither board nor management view strategic thinking as an activity in which one is engaged only from time to time. At all costs, avoid the mindset of the Parisian cat burglar who considered himself a thief only when he was actually stealing.

4. Board committee members rotate often enough to give every director an opportunity to broaden his perspective and deepen his knowledge over time but not so frequently as to threaten continuity. On balance, committee chairmen are rotated less frequently than are committee members.[2]

5. The board meets at least five times a year, once after the end of each quarter, plus one longer, off-site planning session lasting anywhere from one to three days. Between scheduled board meetings, additional meetings are called to deal with important decisions which can't wait or with progress reports on matters of substance or urgency.

Since calendars of busy people fill up months in advance, participation by telephone in meetings called at short notice is not only permissible but used

---

[2] As a rough rule of thumb, committee members might be rotated every three years and committee chairs every five years.

routinely. For information transfer or for decisions where discussion around the board table has taken place earlier, telephonic meetings work fine. For these uses, full attendance by phone is much better than partial attendance in person.

6. For regularly scheduled board meetings, a concerted effort is made both to set dates many months into the future and to try very hard, with both flexibility and patience, to find dates that accommodate the greatest number of directors. This is even more difficult than meets the eye and the bane of executive assistants and board secretaries everywhere and always.

7. The regular board package is in directors' hands at least one full weekend before the board meeting and preferably a full week or more in advance.

   The thickness of the board book follows the Goldilocks model: not too big and not too small but just right. More specifically, it should not confuse nor obfuscate nor intimidate by overload. At the same time, it should not lend credence to the old mushroom theory in which directors are kept in the dark or, slightly less offensively, in the twilight.

8. The board is supported by a senior member of the management team, often both general counsel and corporate secretary. This individual is highly responsive to directors' needs and treats his responsibilities in this area as a central, even predominant, part of his job. The incumbent is someone of stature, someone who enjoys dealing with people, someone who can distinguish in a mature way his responsibilities to the board from those owed to the CEO and to management.

9. One essential role of this person is to maintain, update, and ensure continued board and management buy-in of the roles and responsibilities of the board, the board chairman, the CEO, board committees, and directors. A description of these responsibilities should be kept in writing but must be continually updated to remain useful. And while this paperwork may seem somewhat bureaucratic, continuing review by all concerned helps to minimize ambiguities and potential frictions. It will also help to identify and eliminate functional overlap as well as responsibilities which fall between the stools.

10. Board meetings are highly interactive. Management doesn't talk at directors; previously distributed board materials are not needlessly regurgitated. While knowledge is power, management does not use the obvious reality of much greater in-depth knowledge of the enterprise or of a given topic as a competitive weapon. It does not use this inherent advantage to control the agenda or the discussion. It does not seek to keep the board at arm's length from the locus of power and the real action.

11. The board engages in regular and unblinking self-assessment. Here the role of the chairman is not merely essential, it's crucial. A useful approach is to begin with an annual or no less than biennial questionnaire of modest length but trenchant in its scope, including "sacred cow" issues. This provides a sense of where the board is. This is followed by the chairman meeting with each director individually. The last step is full board discussion led by the chairman armed

with the information he has accumulated plus his own insights.

12. A process is in place for ensuring the replacement of directors who aren't contributing at least at threshold level. Some directors, because of impairment or competing priorities, will recognize the problem and resign of their own volition. Others will need a nudge. Once again, the role of the chairman is crucial.

    Even with such a process in place and working, a compulsory retirement age is also mandated. Retirement begins at the first annual meeting after a director's seventieth birthday. However, I confess that this is one issue on which I'm ambivalent. Is a compulsory retirement age necessary when there is in place an effective process for weeding out non-contributors of any age? Perhaps not. Certainly there are splendid examples of directors making exceptional contributions well into their eighties.

    It's a trade-off. Mandatory age-based retirement means a lamentable loss of wisdom (always a scarce resource) and experience. But there are offsetting advantages in renewal, in fresh thinking and contemporary mind-sets, in belonging to a generation whose network consists primarily of those in power or coming to power instead of those receding from it. And age-based retirement makes the board chairman's job a lot easier.

13. Individual director assessment is never easy. It is potentially both unsettling and divisive. And yet it is necessary. The principle of accountability is universal. Everyone must be accountable to either somebody or

some body. As Mel Brooks used to say, "It's good to be king"...but not for everyone else.

Although in theory there are many possible approaches, few companies use any. Of those who do, almost all go about it very gingerly. The simplest and perhaps best approach—that of our ideal board—is that the board as a whole assesses the non-executive board chairman (as well, of course, as the CEO) and it is the chairman's job to assess each director and to take appropriate action with the support of the rest of the board.

It is belabouring the obvious to observe that directors, people who are more accustomed to assessing than being assessed, should be treated with unusual care and sensitivity. Some observers pooh-pooh this, on the grounds that the sort of people who get to be directors are usually resilient, self-confident, and tough. True to a degree but ego and pride, at least as important, are also involved.

SUMMARY

Do boards exist which meet the admittedly high standards I've tried to describe, if briefly? I believe that they do. In the Canadian setting, I'm familiar with a few which come close. I'm certain there are others. But this is not the norm. Much improvement is possible and needed.

The key question is this: Do ideal boards generate higher returns to shareholders than the rest? There is limited empirical evidence which suggests that they do. But the classic chicken and egg dilemma is at work here. That is, do profitable companies insist on high governance standards (partly because they can afford them) or are high governance standards an important cause of higher profits? It may be a little of each, but my gut instinct and my experience tell me that the second explanation should never, ever, be overlooked or under-weighted.

CHAPTER 2

Board Manners and the Director from Hell

or
Twelve Endearing Ways for New (and Even Some Not-So-New) Directors to Ingratiate Themselves with Fellow Directors and Management

1. At your very first meeting, speak frequently, forcefully, and intrusively. At subsequent meetings, step up the pace.

2. When confronted with the multitude of technical terms and acronyms which are endemic to every industry and company, hide ignorance at all costs. Refuse to ask the CEO or company secretary for a glossary of terms. Muddle through.

3. At about your third board meeting, proclaim loudly that the regular information provided to directors is (a) too voluminous, (b) too sparse, (c) generally off the point and inadequate. Once again, avoid discussing information flow privately with the board chairman and/or the CEO.

4. Communicate regularly on substantive company issues with the CEO's direct reports or even further down the organization. Never tell the CEO what you're doing or obtain his permission to approach his people or even, God forbid, forego the practice.

5. Show up routinely ten or fifteen minutes late for board or committee meetings. Offer no excuses. Or mumble vaguely about deteriorating traffic conditions, execrable weather, or other commitments.

6. At board meetings, address questions to anyone in the room, ignoring the benighted chairman who is striving valiantly to take questions in order and preserve some semblance of organized civility.

7. When discussing potential new board members, advocate vigorously for close friends and colleagues, quite independent of any fit with the background, experience, and qualities needed. Speak out thoughtfully and without prejudice against potential candidates who are (a) female, (b) from a racial minority, (c) from a non-corporate background.

8. Send regularly to the chairman and/or CEO studies and snippets of news about increases in directors' compensation. If asked, talk about the highest-paid board on which you sit or of which you are aware, without reference to comparability.

9. During board discussions, always sit on the edge of your seat, signalling an urgent need to participate. From time to time, interrupt other directors before they've completed their own comments. Make it clear that what you have to say is important and redolent of a vast store of accumulated wisdom.

10. When discussing at board level some important, sub-stantive issue requiring a decision, volunteer your personal experience of fifteen years ago where the differences between the two situations are at least as great as the similarities. Take the time to go into detail; make it clear that the earlier decision was exquisitely correct as demonstrated time and time again over, lo, these many years.

11. When it's clear that, after discussion, the majority of directors disagree with a position you've espoused, never acquiesce gracefully. Either sulk or, better, esca-late the debate in Olympian fashion: *altius, citius, fortius.*

12. If, after displaying for several years many of the endearing qualities or habits described above, you are advised by the chairman that your name will not be on the next slate of directors, don't take it lying down. Fly into a towering rage or threaten legal action (however unlikely to succeed) or both. Demonstrate the inapplicability of Malcolm's unforgettable line to Duncan in MacBeth: "Nothing in his life became him like the leaving it."

Obviously I've exaggerated some annoying or even rep-rehensible traits in order to highlight them; please forgive the hyperbole. I have observed over many years that the great majority of directors, both new and experienced, are courteous and civil. They are acutely aware that a board can work harmoniously, both as a unit and with manage-ment, only if the kinds of excrescences I've described are avoided carefully and fully. So why have I thought it use-ful to enumerate some of them? Because every now and then ....

CHAPTER 3

Things Boards Could Do Better

David Letterman loves to produce lists of one kind or another, as did his predecessor, Johnny Carson. Perhaps it's catching: here are ten things which first-class boards and managements, using leading-edge governance, can and should do better.

1. ADOPT A SENSITIVE, INDIVIDUAL DIRECTOR ASSESSMENT PROGRAM

Individual director assessment has, for good reasons, been a long time coming. I am now convinced that the key to doing it right is peer evaluation. The focus should be developmental, not judgemental. By that I mean that the point of the exercise is not to pass critical, negative judgement on directors, but rather to help them carry out their duties more effectively through positive, constructive criticism. The use of outside consultants to collect, collate, and feed back the data which each director provides via a carefully constructed questionnaire can help to reduce the sensitivities to acceptable levels.

The principal reason for using a consultant is to help ensure total confidentiality as well as to minimize the likelihood of potentially embarrassing interpersonal disagreements. However, it is crucial that control of the entire process remain with the board and not with the consultant or, of course, with management.

The Bank of Montreal is in the vanguard of a small number of companies which are using this aid to better governance. Despite the natural wariness of many companies and boards about tackling this sensitive issue, director evaluation—more specifically, peer evaluation—will almost certainly become more common over the next few years, as I think it should.

2. FOREGO COMPULSORY RETIREMENT FOR DIRECTORS

If peer evaluation is done well, there is probably no need for compulsory retirement. The criterion for retirement at any age becomes measured performance, not an arbitrary and not especially useful number like time spent on earth.

Not all men and women are created equal or, if the U.S. Declaration of Independence is right, they certainly don't develop and grow equally. Some stop learning and growing and contributing at 40. Others are still making significant contributions at 80.

3. SIMPLIFY GOVERNANCE FOR SMALLER COMPANIES

Smaller companies, whether public or private, need governance every bit as much as larger ones. But it's definitely not the same kind of governance. It must be shorn of unnecessary or over-elaborate process. It must focus on a few important fundamentals which can truly help a small company do better, even in the uber-competitive environment, with little margin for error, which so often confronts the entrepreneur and the small businessman.

Avoid detailed procedure manuals, which are as expensive to maintain and keep up to date as to put together in the first place.

Subject to the law and to simple but sound ethical, environmental, and human resource considerations, concentrate on the best interests of shareholders, using as straightforward and unambiguous a strategy as the specifics of a given enterprise permit.

4. EXPECT ALL DIRECTORS TO STAY CURRENT THROUGH ONGOING EDUCATION AND TRAINING

The great myth is that older, more experienced directors don't need any further training or education. Not so. As has so often been said, learning is a journey, not a destination. If it were a destination, you would stop growing when you reached it. And none of us wants to stop growing.

5. DELEGATE CEO SUCCESSION ISSUES TO BOARDS, EVEN WITH 100%-OWNED SUBSIDIARIES

With subsidiary companies, especially when 100%-owned by a parent company or even where there are minority shareholders, there is a common practice which is anything but a best practice. Consider this micro-case study. One morning, the outside chairman of the board of a company with a dominant shareholder located outside Canada reads his copy of an internal memo, noting that the Canadian CEO has been offered and has accepted another position within the corporation in another country. The memo notes that no decision has yet been made about a successor. No previous discussion. No warning. No concession to or recognition of the board's role.

Although it's clear that a parent company holding all of a subsidiary's shares has the right, certainly *de jure*, to remove the CEO of that subsidiary, it would be better if that parent were to eliminate independent directors from its subsidiary's board than to emasculate their role to the point that no advice is sought; in fact, there is no discussion at all.

While the parent company usually and properly wants to arrange subsidiary CEO succession to mesh with its global strategy, surely it would benefit from listening to its independent directors who know the local scene and can comment usefully on local contenders. Often the decision would be the same but sometimes not. At a minimum, the independent directors would feel that their views had been heard and that they had not been disenfranchised.

With a controlling shareholder and a public float, the argument for board involvement is much stronger. In fact, any controlling shareholder which fails to engage fully with its subsidiary board on CEO succession could be exposing itself needlessly to a lawsuit by minority shareholders.

6. DELEGATE THE SELECTION OF NEW DIRECTORS TO BOARD CHAIRMAN AND/OR A BOARD COMMITTEE, EVEN WITH 100%-OWNED SUBSIDIARIES

A somewhat analogous situation arises when a board wishes to replace or add a director. With a controlling shareholder, without or even sometimes with minority shareholders, there is often a tendency to want to manage the process and control the choice, rather than delegate it to a nominating committee of the board where a majority of the members are independent directors.

Once again, this flies in the face of good governance. The signal to the independent directors and to financial markets (there are few things not in the market any more, at least not for long) is that governance doesn't matter. And yet there is a great deal of evidence that good corporate performance and good governance go hand in hand. While cause and effect flow both ways, the latter almost certainly helps to improve the former.

7. USE PERFORMANCE OPTIONS MORE FREQUENTLY AND ROUTINELY

Options provide a useful and tax-efficient way to forge a community of interest among a company's interests and those of its executives. Important as this is, such options should pay out, for the most part, by the amount by which the company's share price increases more than a suitable index of its most comparable peer group. Perhaps one-quarter to one-third of the payout should be based on absolute share price increase and two-thirds to three-quarters on relative share price increase.

Only a few companies use this more demanding regimen. It's not easy to embrace if your competitors provide options of the conventional, more generous kind. But the hard reality is that, in the long bull market which persisted until mid-2000, most options paid off generously for stock price increases which had less to do with executive performance than with largely exogenous factors, such as sharply rising price-earnings ratios.

8. SEPARATE THE ROLES OF BOARD CHAIRMAN AND CEO, EXCEPT IN UNUSUAL CIRCUMSTANCES

The oldest chestnut and yet the most persistent of governance issues is the secular equivalent of the separation of church and state. Should the roles of the board chairman and the CEO be vested in one person or two?

I won't go over old ground except to note that the most compelling argument for separation is that, ideally, a board and a management create a coherent system of checks and balances which provides that well-known creative tension which can and should enhance corporate performance. One person cannot be on both sides of that tension. That's a form of schizophrenia. A lead director can help but it's a palliative at best and a partial substitute for the real thing: genuine role separation.

At the most elementary, even primal level, the issue comes down to power. A management which doesn't want to share power with a board, and is in a position to resist successfully such power-sharing, will insist on the combination of roles. If Lord Acton ("absolute power corrupts absolutely") was right about the result of over-concentrated power, we should at least be wary and sceptical.

9. AS DIRECTORS, SPEAK OUT FRANKLY AND FEARLESSLY, THOUGH CIVILLY, WHEN NECESSARY

When a respected, high-performing CEO makes a major proposal to his or her board, directors always face the classic dilemma: support the CEO on principle and on past performance or speak against the proposal when convinced that it's wiser to reject. The natural inclination to support a CEO with a good, long track record is balanced by the inevitable reality that even the best CEO can be and occasionally is wrong.

For a director with serious doubts about a given project, especially an important one, it's always a tough call to speak out strongly in opposition. That director may be alone in his concerns; ordinarily and on most issues, he doesn't have the background and depth of knowledge which the CEO has. Disturbing the comfortable consensus which usually animates a board creates risks.

None of this should deter a good director from speaking out against what is perceived to be a flawed proposition. Too often, it does. Civility matters; teamwork matters; consensus matters. But making the right decisions on the big, pivotal decision matters more and most.

In 1989, I was a director of Trizec Corporation when we approved a decision to proceed with the massive Bay-Adelaide project. At that board meeting, there was full and informed discussion, followed by full and total consensus. If anyone in that boardroom had qualms, they were not articulated.

In our collective defence, 1989 and the several prior years saw a strong, even ebullient economy, especially in Toronto. It would have been difficult and have required more prescience than most of us fallible mortals possess to foretell the harsh recession which was soon to follow and that the sector most severely affected would be real estate.

In the event, construction began; excavation and a large parking garage were completed. And a concrete-encased elevator shaft rises seven stories above ground as a monument to the sharp real estate recession of the early nineties, which brought the project to a halt. It is still on hold today in early 2002.

10. AS DIRECTORS, AVOID POTENTIAL, LET ALONE ACTUAL, CONFLICTS OF INTERESTS

Directors always have a potential conflict of interest when they sit on the board of a company and also do business or try to do business with that company, either as an individual or as the representative of another organization. Granted, it may translate into an actual conflict only infrequently, especially if the director is able to and does distance himself personally from any business relationship. But at least occasionally, a situation arises which is awkward for everyone concerned. And it's usually difficult to resolve amicably, economically, and with good governance intact.

Despite certain practical offsets (a director's firm may go the extra mile to perform well), it's better on the whole not to have to face this situation at all.

CHAPTER 4

Ten Best Practices of Modern Corporate Governance

In the practice of corporate governance in the modern, director-proactive era, there are many imbedded concepts and ideals which have come, in an evolutionary way, to be accepted by most reasonable persons as sound and useful. Several thousand words could be devoted to any one of them and I will discuss each of them and others in more detail later in this book. For now, my purpose is simply to list several of them and to provide a personal assessment of best practice.

1. Every director of a public company should own stock in that company. This is not merely desirable; it is essential. The optimum amount will vary and so will the time needed to reach it. The range of minimum acceptable ownership is three to seven times annual retainer; up to five years is an acceptable period to get there.

   Does this discriminate against less-wealthy directors? At least in theory, it does, although the problem can be lessened by various forms of assistance such as loan programs.

2. Directors buying shares should hold them until retirement. Exceptions can be made for financial exigencies. Though some boards follow this practice, it is honoured in the breach as much as in the observance. When I read insider trading reports showing directors selling, I cringe at the signal to the market. Directors must not be fair-weather shareholders. And speculation in a director's company's shares is, of course, beyond the pale.

3. A stock grant should be an integral part of director compensation, regardless of how much personal stock any director already holds. At least one-third of the annual retainer should be in shares at market price. Directors should also be given the opportunity to take up to 100% of their retainer in shares.

4. Companies with stock option plans for directors should at least encourage and preferably require that at least half of the after-tax gain on options exercised be retained in company shares and held to retirement.

5. Option plans have recently been getting a bad press in some circles but, so long as the value of a company's total compensation package for directors is fair (i.e., market-competitive), an option component makes sense, especially in the context of what was said in point four.

   It may be true that, in a strong bull market, an option is, as Warren Buffet described, "a royalty on the passage of time." But we live in a cyclical world economy. Bull markets end and are followed by less benign periods when the gain from an option is earned the hard way if it is earned at all.

   For the most part, critics of option plans are concerned less about the principle than about the egregious and extraordinary amounts granted routinely to senior executives and occasionally to directors.

6. On the repricing of options, my view is simplicity itself: never, never, never. Perhaps there is a circumstance when repricing is acceptable but I can't think of one, though I've tried.

   Could I be persuaded that supply and demand considerations for executives, especially in industries where cash is in short supply, should override my basic aversion to repricing? Perhaps, although I remind myself that the shareholder who bought his shares at market doesn't get this second chance.

7. With globalization, citizens of other countries, especially the U.S., are sought increasingly as directors of Canadian companies with international operations or aspirations. Such directors should be paid at precisely the same scale as a Canadian director. Travel allowances

are acceptable but only if based on distance or time and offered to all directors.

For a Canadian company to pay a U.S. director the same number of U.S. dollars that a Canadian director receives in Canadian dollars is unfair and wrong-headed. If fees are insufficient to attract a U.S. director, it may be necessary to raise all fees, but all directors should be paid the same in whatever currency, usually Canadian dollars, a company chooses. Any fee increases required are part of the price of internationalization. The alternative of valuing the services of one class of directors at a higher rate than another is unacceptable and insulting to Canadian directors.

8. The concept of lead director is a palliative, a second-best solution. It's a band-aid alternative to the separation of the roles of board chairman and CEO. On the whole, it works best in those situations where the roles are separated but both the chairman and the CEO are part of the management structure. This is often found in a conglomerate or in a holding company/operating company structure. That is, the chairman represents the interests of the controlling or significant shareholder and the CEO is the senior officer of the controlled entity. In this situation, a truly independent lead director can play a useful, if limited, role.

Nor has the concept caught on much in boards where the roles of the chairman and the CEO are combined. In this situation, a lead director fulfills part but not all of the job of chairman. This can lead to ambiguity and confusion between the two roles.

Reflecting this lack of clarity is the fact that the lead director job is usually not valued highly in compensation terms.

In this country, the mainstream direction is separation of roles. The board chairman has carriage of oversight and governance; the CEO manages the business and answers to the shareholders through the board and its chairman. In a somewhat different context, this is also the preferred model in the U.K. In the U.S., the roles are combined in something like 80% of Fortune 500 companies, leaving the real power with management.

9. Constituency boards, in which one or more directors represent a specific interest-group constituency (e.g., a labour union) in addition to the enterprise and its shareholders, are, despite an occasional exception, usually failed experiments. All directors must, of course, pursue single-mindedly the best interests of the corporation and its shareholders, not the best interests of some other stakeholder or constituency. A constituency director always faces this unhappy choice: act like other directors and disappoint his constituency or flout convention and create divisiveness, impeding effective governance.

10. Finally, there's director retirement. Should it be mandated at some age or be discretionary at the call of the chair and/or a board committee (like nominating)? While this issue is black and white, I believe[1] that a fixed-age retirement policy is, on balance, the poorer choice.

---

[1] On Mondays, Wednesdays, and Fridays. On Tuesdays and Thursdays, I lean the other way.

Granted, it's easier on the chairman to avoid or at least delay sensitive decisions on who, post-cutoff age, is worth retaining and who isn't. But it suffers from two serious flaws. First, it weakens the resolve to retire directors who are well below the cutoff age but who are not contributing and should be replaced. ("Heck: Charley's only five years from retirement. Let's not rock the boat.") Second, it prevents the retention of directors—admittedly there are not a huge number of them—who have more wisdom and smarts at 80 than others have at 50.

Some Personal Experiences as a Director
(I)

When I write or speak about corporate governance and board performance—and I do my share of it—I usually deal with principles and rules of conduct and trends of one kind or another.

The last time I spoke on this topic, a couple of months ago, a member of the audience came up to me afterwards and said "You've sat on a lot of boards over the course of your career. Why don't you talk more about some of your actual experiences, tell some war stories? And name names."

That kind of hit home to me. I have sat on a lot of boards, dating back thirty-nine years to 1963. In fact, when I went to the trouble of toting up the numbers, I was mildly surprised to find that I've sat on 50 corporate boards, of which 17 were job-related and 33 were not; that is, I was an independent director. I have also served on another 40 not-for-profit boards (or their equivalent), but their grist is for the mill of another day.

In several sections of this book, I'm going to recount personal anecdotes that span those many years and, with each of them, I'll try to draw a lesson, something I learned from each experience, for better or for worse.

One of the very first boards on which I was invited to serve as an independent director shall be left nameless for reasons which will be apparent in a moment. I was invited by the company's CEO, whom I had known from a trade association to which we both belonged, to join his company's board. But a week before my first board meeting, he had begun an unplanned leave of absence due to a serious illness. As it happened, he never returned.

When I arrived at the appointed hour for that first meeting, the directors—there were thirteen of us in all; I knew two of them slightly—assembled in an anteroom outside the boardroom proper for a morning coffee or tea and biscuits. Soon we all moved into a large, formal chamber with oil portraits of former chairmen and CEOs adorning the panelled walls.

I saw that a name card sat in front of each director and I quickly learned that the custom, which probably went back a century to the company's origins, was for the director with the most seniority to sit closest to the chairman at one end of a very long, very polished table. As seniority lessened, the distance increased. I found my name card at the bottom of the table, some thirty feet from the chairman and sat down meekly.

After the chairman and the corporate secretary had exchanged formal niceties about appointing each of them to their respective posts for the purpose of the meeting at hand, and had articulated the usual legalities about "proper notice having been given" and "we do have a properly constituted forum," the meeting commenced. The chairman put down the paper from which he had been intoning, removed his glasses carefully, and, looking down the long table at me, said solemnly: "Welcome, Mr. Dimma, to your first board meeting. I'm sure you'll find this a most interesting board. There is only one thing I wish to say to you. It is and, for many years, has been our custom that a new director is not expected to speak during his first year of board service." I nodded blankly.

The lesson? Governance has changed quite a lot, perhaps even profoundly, over the past few decades. And, if I may say so, thank God for such mercies.

The first board I joined which was related to my employment was that of Union Carbide Canada Limited. It was 1966; I was 37 years old. I had just been appointed the company's executive vice-president along with an invitation to become a director. The board was chaired by my boss, Jack Dewar, the company's chairman, president, and CEO.

A couple of years earlier, Union Carbide Canada Limited had become a public company. In response to a Canadianization incentive program introduced by Walter Gordon, then the Minister of Finance, Carbide did an IPO, the largest in Canadian history at that point in time, selling 25% of its equity to the Canadian public.

With only six directors, the board was small. However, the members, beside my boss and me, were a formidable quartet:

- Ben Benedict was second in command of the global parent company, Union Carbide Corporation.

- Senator Salter Hayden headed the law firm McCarthy & McCarthy, as well as the Finance Committee of the Canadian Senate.

- Allen Lambert was Chairman, President and CEO of the T-D Bank.

- Ian Sinclair was Chairman and CEO of Canadian Pacific Railway.

The lesson is that it's often salutary to run a little scared. And moving in fast company helps fast learning.

In the second half of the 1970s, I sat on the boards of Torstar Corporation and its wholly owned subsidiary, Toronto Star Newspapers Limited. From 1974 to 1976, I sat as an independent director, then from mid-1976 to the end of 1979 as an employee, as president of both companies.

Both then and now, these organizations were effectively controlled by a voting trust. It included the shares of the founding Atkinson family, the Atkinson Foundation, and four other large shareholders: the Hindmarsh, Campbell, Honderich, and Thall families.

When I joined the board, it included two octogenarians and two septuagenarians, along with a few others of less advanced age.

Later, and before the deaths of Bill Campbell and Ruth Hindmarsh, the daughter of founder Joe Atkinson, the board included one centenarian, one nonagenarian, and two young bucks in their seventies. And yet, despite what you might think, this board functioned very effectively indeed during both my tenure and later.

There are two lessons here. The first is that having large ownership blocs represented on boards is not only mete and just, but often such boards function at least as well as and sometimes better than boards made up of independent directors, each with only modest shareholdings.

The second lesson, if I can wax poetic for a moment, is contained in Shakespeare's well-worn line: "Age cannot wither, nor custom stale her infinite variety." Remove the gender bias and the Bard underscores the growing realization that a lot of wisdom need not be discarded indiscriminately by arbitrary mandatory retirement rules. Sitting on boards is not like digging ditches or carrying bricks in large hods.

PART 2

Getting in Gear: How to Make it Work

CHAPTER 5

Board and Director Evaluation

One of the few downsides of trying to improve corporate governance is the risk that process will dominate substance and results, an endemic problem in every field of human endeavour. Nevertheless, board and director evaluation—essentially a process issue—is important.

At the most elemental level, it's important because, in a democracy, every institution and every individual should be—must be—accountable. History is on the side of those who believe that, while untempered authority sometimes produces efficiency, the side effects are invariably negative, sometimes devastatingly so.

In the business world, people and functions report through a management hierarchy to a CEO who reports to a board, ideally but not always through a separate chairman. The board reports, through the chairman, to the shareholders. The CEO holds the senior management group accountable, collectively, and individually, and this accountability principle permeates the organization. The board holds the CEO accountable. The shareholders hold the board accountable. All basic stuff.

But there's a rub. This last link in the accountability chain is usually tenuous; in most large, publicly held companies the shareholders are numerous, disparate, and rarely organized to play a meaningful role in the chain of accountability. Occasionally, an institutional investor, by virtue of size and conviction, will take a stand but usually only after a problem of some consequence has reared its head.

A board that regularly and routinely assesses performance—of the organization, of itself, and of its members—can anticipate and head off or at least minimize problems rather than have to deal with them later in their development and sometimes too late.

What areas are most suitable for assessment? The list is potentially endless but should include the following:

- appropriate board agenda items,
- frequency and length of meetings,
- role and number of board committees,
- director selection, compensation, retirement,
- quality of board-level discussion. (Focused? Insightful?),
- relationship between board and CEO (Is there creative tension? Mutual respect? Is it neither adversarial nor superficial nor muddled?),

- role of board in strategy formulation,
- adequacy of information flow,
- role of board in senior management development, evaluation, succession,
- evaluation of CEO performance,
- evaluation of board chairman performance,
- evaluation of collective board performance,
- evaluation of individual director performance.

As is evident, this incomplete list is made up of categories of process. It doesn't attempt to list any of a vast array of substantive issues which, though important and sometimes urgent, are situationally determined.

On board performance, there are various approaches in common use. One is a written questionnaire. I've seen them from one to thirty pages, from rambling to incisive, from exquisite detail to floating above the issues. A well-drafted questionnaire that homes in on issues specific to a given board, i.e., that is tailored to a board's culture, practices, expectations, and current issues, provides a reasonable starting point.

Usually the completed questionnaires are then aggregated, distributed to board members in advance, and discussed at board level. This is sometimes done at the end of a regular board meeting, often at the last meeting of a fiscal year. Or it can be at a special meeting called for the sole purpose of evaluating performance.

Sometimes an intermediate step is taken, after the questionnaire but prior to full board discussion. That is, the chairman meets with each director individually, encouraging him to expand on areas of concern and perhaps to say things he might not wish to put in writing. Some boards omit the questionnaire altogether and rely heavily on the personal, one-on-one interview, which can be as structured or unstructured as the chairman wishes.

Occasionally a consultant is used to conduct the interviews, but I think this is less effective than if the chairman does it. What is gained in professional interviewing technique is more than offset by lack of knowledge of the nuances of a particular board and by introducing a stranger as middleman into a set of personal dynamics.

Still another approach to board assessment, largely untried but broached occasionally, is to use the external auditors to do the job. My first reaction is that accounting firms would need to provide a great deal of special training to ready them for this task. A more basic concern is that, since boards are involved in the auditor selection process as well as in approving audit fees, the potential for conflict is considerable.

Individual director assessment is a touchy topic but, despite the obvious sensitivities, it is a concept whose time had finally arrived. The principle of accountability, which is individual as well as collective, demands it.

The difficulties inherent in evaluating the performance of people who are usually successful, proud, high achievers in their own right, and far more accustomed to assessing than being assessed are not inconsiderable. But the process can be brought into a manageable range by how the job is done. The devil, as usual, is in the details.

It is more likely to be useful and successful if the purpose is both clear and well communicated and, as mentioned earlier, if that purpose is principally developmental (i.e., to help improve individual director performance and, as a consequence, collective board performance), rather than judgemental. In short, the principal focus should be on the identification of problems and on appropriate remedial action, whether it's counselling, education or training, a word to the wise, or even, in extremis, a "woodshed" session.

The role of the chairman in this delicate area is crucial and he needs the finesse of a diplomat much more than the usual attributes of a prosecuting attorney (or hanging judge).

What is not likely to become best practice is the notion of directors rating one another. If they are critical (even anonymously) of one or more of their colleagues, damage is done to "the cohesion and sense of equality that is so crucial to effective boards," as Harvard's Jay Lorsch once phrased it. More likely, directors will spare one another out of innate civility or perhaps because if "we don't hang together, we'll all hang separately." A rare exception is the case of a director who is well beyond the pale but, in such a case, the chairman hardly needs the advice of other directors.

A somewhat more effective approach is to ask the nominating or corporate governance committee to evaluate each director prior to his renomination. There are two problems with this. First, who evaluates the evaluators? Second, renomination in the Canadian setting is annual; longer terms are the exception.

Probably the best approach is for the chairman (or lead director if the CEO is also chairman) to undertake this necessary but thankless task.[1]

---

[1] As an irrelevant and irreverent aside, a senior federal official once referred in a private meeting to the Canadian Senate as a taskless thanks.

It's clear that the task of identifying underperforming directors is fraught with difficulty. Who should be counseled? Who should be advised that renomination is not on? Or is it wiser to let age-determined retirement solve the problem? Is this pusillanimous or is valour the worse part of discretion?

It seems to me that, in a performance-dominated era, doing nothing about something which detracts from performance is, to use that stern phrase from the military, a dereliction of duty. And that's unacceptable. But governance is still feeling its way as it attempts to define best practice in this area.

Advisory Boards

This chapter presents briefly the pros and cons of fully constituted boards versus advisory boards for the wholly owned Canadian subsidiaries of foreign corporations.

The advisory board concept has a number of advantages. From the perspective of the Canadian director, directors' liabilities are essentially eliminated. From the viewpoint of the Canadian subsidiary, an advisory board clarifies the issue of to whom the subsidiary CEO is truly responsible, although frankly there's not much doubt in most cases. Just answer the question "Who decides the Canadian CEO's compensation?" and you've clarified where responsibilities and allegiances lie. The occasional exception is where the Canadian board chairman is a strong personality and the Canadian CEO is influenced by greater day-to-day contact with that chairman than with his "real" boss hundreds or thousands of miles away.

The disadvantages of advisory boards include the fact that the Canadian CEO loses the ability to use a real board as a bogeyman to spur on performance and to push his people to meet deadlines. The image of a tough, demanding taskmaster is harder to sustain with an advisory board.

Also, a real board makes directors feel like and act like directors. They are more likely to take their responsibilities more seriously, those responsibilities being greater in any event.

Finally, and this is, I think, the strongest point, real boards help to protect the public interest more than advisory boards. A real board, the majority of whose members are Canadian residents (that, I realize, is an issue in itself)[1], is much more likely to speak up on topics where the public interest is involved than an advisory board which typically provides advice, when asked, in areas put forward by either local management or senior representatives of the foreign parent.

That is, a member of a regular board has clear responsibilities to all shareholders, including any minority shareholders. This should encourage him to speak out on sensitive, even controversial, issues where the public interest and that of the controlling shareholder may differ. An advisory board member is, as I said, more likely to comment on such issues only if asked. He is in the boardroom more as a consultant than as a member of a body with regulatory responsibilities and a certain amount of clout.

---

[1] An amendment on November 24, 2001 to the Canada *Business Corporations Act* reduces the Canadian residency requirements, in most cases, from a majority to 25%.

But the ledger has two sides. Technically, economically, practically, the advisory board concept works just fine when there are no minority shareholders. The corporation (that is, both the foreign parent and the local subsidiary) gets what it wants: advice as requested in areas like local political and economic conditions, as well as door-openings from time to time, but with minimal interference with the omnipresent global mandate. I'm convinced that, with free trade, global strategies, and globalization, the clear and growing trend to advisory boards will continue.

I have chaired two companies which are 100% owned by foreign parents, one in Europe, one in the U.S. Both parents are large corporations with increasingly well-conceived and well-articulated global strategies. Both Canadian subsidiaries are themselves large, at least by Canadian standards. One did have and one still does have regularly constituted boards, if for no other reason than regulatory requirements and constraints. From a practical operational perspective, I don't doubt that advisory boards would serve the corporate interest reasonably well.

If present trends continue, I believe that the advisory board structure might easily become the dominant form for 100% foreign-controlled Canadian companies. Would this be a good thing or not? Opinion is divided. On balance I believe this issue provides one further small example of the migration of economic power or at least influence to foreign jurisdictions. Perhaps this is inevitable, but as a personal aside, I believe it's probably contrary to the long-run Canadian public interest, though this is too large and separate a topic to dwell on here.

MORE ON ADVISORY BOARDS

In the evolution of corporate governance, we are seeing more advisory boards in North America as well as wider uses for them.

Let me begin by describing the more common configurations. With public companies, a conventional regular board is sometimes supplemented by either a single national advisory board or by several concurrent regional advisory boards (sometimes named advisory councils). Less common in public companies is the use of advisory boards comprising external members, operating concurrently with a regular board made up, to the greatest extent legally possible, of internal directors. For obvious reasons, the minority shareholders are not well served by this arrangement.

Advisory boards are more frequently used in private companies. The three most prevalent scenarios are these:

1. A wholly owned subsidiary of a foreign corporation often needs and wants independent, external advice on domestic politics, expected economic conditions, and markets. Or it wants door-openers and public association with well-connected, high-profile Canadians.

    What a global corporation does not want or need is "meddling" with the Canadian component of its global strategy, determined and monitored at world headquarters. And as the sole shareholder of that subsidiary, it is free to rely on and does rely on its own management and staff for crucial functions like setting goals, vetting performance, and the placement/displacement of senior subsidiary management.

2. A Canadian company is contemplating the transition from private to public status. This is often a young company with aggressive growth aspirations and pressing needs for new capital. In this situation, it is far-sighted and fairly common to put an advisory board in place to help steer the transition. Subsequently, a regular board is elected with the headstart advantage of having a cadre of suitable directors in place.

3. Finally, there is the private company owned by an individual or small group or other company and with every intention of remaining private. The controlling shareholder(s) recognizes the need for independent counsel on an ongoing basis but wishes to minimize the "rigmarole" of full and formal governance, i.e., the inconvenience and cost of the bureaucratic trappings which seem, inevitably, to accompany regular boards.

Turning to the specific uses to which advisory boards are put, I find that these are wider today than even five years ago and include the following:

1. Well-known and respected businessmen (and women) on advisory boards bring credibility, contacts, and the ability to facilitate an introduction and a hearing.

2. By recruiting people who might be unconventional candidates for regular boards, companies can often gain fresh insights and "outside the box" thinking on emerging or unfamiliar or intransigent issues.

Candidates for regular boards tend to come from a rather narrow gene pool[2], although suggestions that this should be broader are on the increase.

Advisory boards accommodate and even welcome individuals with much more varied background and who are more representative of society as a whole. Examples might include an artist on the board of an advertising agency; a football player, active or retired, on the board of an athletic equipment company; or a craftsman on the board of a furniture manufacturing company.

3. Experience without the baggage of any controlling or judgmental aspect can be brought to bear on a broad array of issues, such as:

- a company is re-evaluating its basic vision, mission, and/or strategy,

- it is considering a major restructuring or it wishes to reposition itself in its market,

- it wants to enter a new business or a new market or introduce a new product,

- it plans to go global,

- it needs to deal with new technology,

- it is facing an impending competitive threat,

- it seeks advice on national or regional political, economic, market issues,

---

[2] This pool is made up primarily of active or retired senior executives plus a sprinkling of professionals (mostly lawyers), retired politicians, and academics, notably university presidents, active or retired, and distinguished members of professional faculties.

- it wants the views of women, minorities, and/or relevant special interest groups on matters of ongoing importance to it.

As mentioned earlier, an advisory board can be a preparatory stage towards a regular board. Where an advisory board and a regular board co-exist, the former can provide a candidate pool for the latter. An advisory board is not incidentally, a single-purpose focus group brought together for a limited time to deal with a defined problem.

For both companies and individuals, there are, of course, advantages and disadvantages to advisory boards vis-à-vis full boards. For companies, the pluses include these:

- Management is not constrained by the requirements of a regular board with full oversight responsibilities. The focus is on non-binding advice, not on control, approvals, and governance.

- The all-in cost is lower. Furthermore, advisory boards often provide valuable advice at a much lower cost than that provided by consultants. This assumes the right membership: independent thinkers, creative strategists, people with extensive knowledge of and experience in the industry.

- The format is flexible and can be tailored easily to the specific needs of a given company. How it's structured is crucial. As always, God (or the devil) is in the details.

- It's easier to change or add members. Usually, appointments are for a one-year or, at most, two-year term.

The two main disadvantages are these:

1. Where there is both a fully independent regular board and an advisory board, there is the potential for overlap and confusion, or at least ambiguity. However, this can largely be controlled if the ground rules are clear and well maintained.

2. The creative tension and separation of roles of board and management which accompany a fully independent regular board are, of course, lost with the alternative combination of an advisory board and a largely inside regular board.

For the individual, the advisory board entails few, if any, legal liabilities. It provides an opportunity to offer advice in a free-wheeling, more flexible, less structured format, with emphasis on the big picture, not on the minutiae with which even the best regular boards are inevitably saddled. The time commitment is less but so is the compensation, not only per annum but also in dollars per hour of time required.

In summary, advisory boards can add value under the right circumstances. In private companies, they can provide all of whatever input from independent directors is wanted, without the need to worry about governance issues. In public companies, advisory boards can be useful adjuncts to regular boards.

But for a public company to replace a regular board which has a strong representation of independent directors with the combination of an advisory board and a regular board comprising primarily of insiders is ill advised. It encourages governance of the worst kind.

To flesh out some of these concepts with some short case histories, let me offer four examples of advisory boards where I've been involved. Consider, first, Royal LePage, where I have chaired three consecutive iterations of a commercial real estate advisory board. In the early '90s, the company concerned itself with the Greater Toronto Region. From about 1996 on, it broadened its scope to cover all of Canada. And from mid-2000 forward, it has once again shifted its focus to Ontario.

Until a little more than a year ago, Royal LePage, as a public company, had a regular board with several independent directors. But in 1999, Trilon, which became the controlling shareholder in 1984, bought out the public's minority shares and disbanded its regular board. However, this had no impact on the commercial advisory board.

This advisory group has several purposes:

• to open client doors at senior levels,

• to provide advice from time to time on commercial real estate issues,

• to encourage, via various business/social functions, the mingling of well-known business leaders who sit on the advisory board with the Royal LePage commercial sales force and sales management.

My second example is Monsanto Canada. For many years, the company had a regular board with full responsibilities, three board committees and four independent directors, as well as two directors from Monsanto Corporation and the two senior officers of the Canadian company. I chaired this board for about seven years.

In 1997, the regular board was replaced with an advisory board, consistent with my earlier comments about the nuisance created by regular boards meddling in some or other aspect of global strategy.

There were four roles assigned to this body. These were:

1. to open doors at the federal and provincial government levels with both politicians and senior bureaucrats,

2. to help provide a better understanding of the Canadian and regional environment and economy,

3. to provide an unbiased and independent reaction to new product initiatives, especially in the pharmaceutical and biotech sectors,

4. and, finally, to help deal with such controversial public relations issues as the use of BST to stimulate milk production from cows or the use of genetically modified foods.

As a matter of incidental interest, Monsanto eliminated its advisory board and all outside representation at the end of 1998. At that time and since, there were a lot of major changes taking place in Monsanto globally. Earlier this year, Monsanto Corporation of St. Louis, Mo., was acquired by Pharmacia Upjohn, now known as Pharmacia. This came after Monsanto's earlier unsuccessful attempt to merge with American Home Products.

My third example is more recent and quite different. A group of bright, energetic, young entrepreneurs with excellent technical backgrounds decided over a year ago to start a new business.

The concept was simple. Many U.S. catalogue companies sell to Canadians. Why not build a large fulfillment centre north of the border to serve as many of these U.S. retailers as possible? The advantage for them would be better service and lower cost through outsourcing to an on-site facility in Toronto, where a good segment of the market is located.

The new enterprise intended to hold goods on consignment and then fill orders faster and more efficiently than any one U.S. catalogue house can service Canadian orders that involve customs paperwork, duties, sales taxes, the need for prompt delivery, and the ability to handle returns expeditiously.

These young entrepreneurs were smart enough to realize that they needed advice and counsel on a wide range of business issues from older, experienced directors. And so they recruited six or seven greybeards, including me, to form an advisory board.

Their plan was to take the company public, when feasible, and to convert the advisory board to a regular board at that time. The job of recruiting directors for a public company board would, of course, have already been done.[3]

Recently, I had a call from an old friend about the possibility of joining the advisory board of an enterprise in a segment of the high-tech industry. This company, currently private, has been operating for a few years. More recently, it developed a unique software system. The sales forecast for the next four or five years is encouragingly bullish. Director compensation is similar to how high-tech companies tend to pay their executives. That is, there are no

---

[3] Sadly, the economic showdown which began with the new millenium prevented the company from raising the capital necessary to proceed.

directors' fees, only expenses. The attraction is a generous option allocation at a very low price.

Each of these four cases illustrates, I think, some aspect of what I discussed earlier in more general terms. So theory and practice match, at least for the most part.

Board Responsibilities

This chapter and the next will discuss a range of central board responsibilities and issues, commencing with one of the more contentious questions of all for anyone who believes in the value of boards and the efficacy of good corporate governance.

BOARD CHAIRMAN AND CEO ROLES: SEPARATION OR NOT?

So here we go again on that old chestnut about whether or not the board chairman and the CEO roles should be vested in the same person. As with many facets of governance, it's useful, for purposes of analysis, to divide profit-making corporations into three categories:

1. The company is owned 100% by a parent company.

2. The company has a control group but is public with minority shareholders.

3. The company is widely held, with no control group.

Let's consider each of these categories in turn:

1. With *100%-owned companies*, the issue of separation of roles is not important. The parent company calls most of the shots that matter and often wishes to have one of its representatives chair the board. I see no problem with this.

   As a sidebar comment, the strong trend in Canada, under existing free trade arrangements and in the face of massive globalization, is for Canadian subsidiaries of foreign parents to move away from boards to advisory boards or even to no outside director involvement at all, using a bare-bones inside board.

2. With *public companies* with both a control group and minority shareholders, it goes without saying that minority rights must be respected and protected. At least in theory, the CEO who is also board chairman can manage the potential conflict. In practice, this is difficult. Usually the CEO is chosen by the parent, though formally ratified by the board. His compensation, his promotion potential, his very tenure, are influenced heavily, if not actually determined, by parent company management.

Should a situation arise in which there is a conflict or potential conflict between the rights of the majority and those of the minority, a fully independent chairman is better able to steer the board along the right course. Granted, this situation will likely arise only infrequently but, when it does, it is crucial that it be dealt with in a neutral, even-handed way.

To be fair, most control groups are sensitive about doing the right thing. But, as in so many other aspects of life in a sceptical and litigious world, perception is as important as reality.

3. With *widely held companies*, the question of separation of roles is really about the allocation of power and where it ought best to reside. There isn't a majority versus minority shareholder issue. Instead there's a board/management issue.

   In Canada, the consensus (though not unanimous) view is that a widely held company will perform best for its shareholders if the roles of chairman and CEO are separated. There are two issues here: efficiency and effectiveness.

   On the first of these, role separation allows the chairman to focus on the board and its members, on sound corporate governance, and on orchestrating that essential broad overview and reasoned second opinion by (ideally) a group of seasoned and experienced board members. This frees the CEO to manage the company. Of course, some responsibilities will normally be shared—like determining and updating vision, mission, and strategy, like senior management succession, and like safeguarding fiscal probity and prudence.

Many informed persons believe that this division of effort is more efficient than the alternative of combining the roles and that this benefits the shareholder. That is, the CEO who is also board chairman may face too broad a range of duties. Not surprisingly, he will tend to focus on managing the business and perhaps underplay or even neglect sound governance.

The second issue revolves around the question of power. Once again, many believe that a corporation will perform best if power is distributed between the board and management and if there is a creative tension between the CEO, to whom the organization answers, and the board chairman and board, to whom the CEO answers and who answers in turn to the shareholders.

Of course, it's not quite this neat and simple in practice. At times and in some areas, responsibilities blur. For example, the CEO also reports to shareholders directly via quarterly and annual reports, at annual meetings, and in regular interaction with institutional investors.

Despite some blurring at the edges, there is broad support in the Canadian context for the two-person chairman-CEO model. This, as I say, is the conventional wisdom with which I'm in general agreement. Most conventional wisdom is none the less wise for being conventional. Most, but not all. Certainly any fair-minded observer of the corporate scene would want to see and examine some hard evidence before coming to a firm conclusion. Are there any comprehensive studies which compare the profitability over five or, better, ten years of similar companies with a single board chairman/CEO with those where the roles are divided? If there are, I'm not aware of them.

And in any event, there is the formidable, perhaps insurmountable, problem of isolating the influence of one variable on company performance while neutralizing the effect of the myriad of other variables which influence performance profoundly.

There is one comparison—simplistic though it is—which can be made. Something like 75% to 80% of the S&P 500 companies in the U.S. combine the roles of board chairman and CEO in one person. Something like 70% to 75% of the TSE 300 companies in Canada separate the roles. Over most periods ranging from one to twenty-five years, U.S. share performance has been better, usually significantly better, than Canadian share performance. The exception is the period from late 1999 through to the end of 2000.

Are we comparing apples and oranges, that is, the larger, more robust, more diversified, more dynamic U.S. environment with its still somewhat resource-heavy Canadian counterpart? Or do Americans know something we don't? Is it possible, contrary to the prevailing orthodoxy, at least as espoused in Canada and the U.K., that concentration of power at the top is more likely to generate better share performance in the long run than the division of power?

For most of those concerned with good corporate governance, even asking the question goes against the grain. But corporate governance is a process, not a result. It is and must always be a means, never an end. The end is improved corporate performance and return to investors. I'll return to this topic later.

CEO SUCCESSION PLANNING

Before getting into the substance of this topic, I'd like, as with the previous discussion of chairman/CEO role separation, to categorize companies by the nature of their share ownership. This is because succession planning varies with how the shares are held.

Wholly Owned Companies

The first category is wholly-owned companies, usually subsidiaries of parent companies which are frequently headquartered in another country.

The next variable is whether or not the wholly owned subsidiary has a board with independent directors. As the result of globalization and NAFTA, more and more wholly owned, foreign-owned subsidiaries are moving in the direction of advisory boards or advisory councils.

More and more large corporations operating across many borders and in many political jurisdictions have been freed over the past decade or so by various international trade agreements, like NAFTA, from the traditional constraints of trade-inhibiting tariffs and other regulatory impediments.

As a consequence, they have gravitated in an evolutionary way to global strategies determined at the corporate centre. A regular board with its monitoring responsibilities can be an obstacle in the way to achieving the considerable synergies which a global strategy can provide.

That is, from the perspective of the corporate centre, too much emphasis can be placed on the best interests of the subsidiary company in a host country as opposed to the best interests of the globally oriented parent company. An advisory board deals with this issue simply and, for the most part, effectively.

With large diversified transnationals and multinationals with coherent global strategies, the head of each product-market or individual business in a country like Canada reports normally to the head of that same business globally and who's most likely located at world headquarters.

In a more secondary and sometimes even peripheral sense, he reports to the CEO of the Canadian subsidiary. The role of such a CEO is, more and more, that of a senior lobbyist.

I won't dwell further on this category of company except to say that the appointment of the CEO is primarily a matter for the management of the global corporation to determine and that any appointment should be fully congruent with the imperatives and priorities of global strategy.

Legally Constituted Board

Now let's move to the situation where the wholly owned Canadian subsidiary of a global corporation does have a legally constituted board with several independent directors. When the time comes to appoint a new CEO, the usual process is that someone in the parent company simply advises board members that, as of some near-future date, the corner office will have a new occupant.

At first blush, this seems arbitrary—but consider further. Since strategy is global and is determined elsewhere, the board of the Canadian sub isn't much involved in formulating that strategy though it is, of course, involved in strategy implementation.

Since the deployment of senior people throughout a global corporation must serve a global strategy, the management of the parent company usually believes, not surprisingly, that the appointment of a subsidiary CEO, a country CEO, is entirely a parent-level responsibility.

The existence of a subsidiary board with independent directors makes little difference (nor should it) to the substance of the CEO succession process.

It may, however, make some difference to the etiquette of the process. It's not unusual for the outside chairman of the wholly owned Canadian subsidiary to journey to global headquarters to meet the proposed CEO before it's official. Often, this is a formality. But even when the outside chairman's view is genuinely sought, what can he say or do, since it's rational and reasonable that global strategy should be served?

But suppose there's a bright, young, high-potential person in the Canadian operation whom the outside chairman and the independent directors have come to know and respect and who appears ready to take on the CEO challenge. And suppose the parent company proposes someone else, someone from within the corporation but from outside the Canadian subsidiary. Here the chairman might be emboldened to ask a few pointed questions. However, he can only push so far; lack of knowledge is lack of power.

Furthermore, the global corporation, with a sophisticated management succession planning process in place and functioning well, is likely to have other plans for the young contender, designed to broaden his international experience and enhance his career potential.

Controlling Shareholder

The next category is a public company with a controlling shareholder, usually another corporation, but with lots of minority shareholders and shares listed on a public stock exchange. In this situation, the independent directors and management have a responsibility to all of the shareholders, including a clear one to the minority shareholders, to ensure that the best available CEO is appointed.

Whether the parent company is foreign or Canadian, a conglomerate or a multinational, it will still likely want to appoint someone to support a global strategy. But in this situation it's highly dubious in governance terms when the parent makes the CEO appointment unilaterally. Nevertheless, this is what happens all too often. The parent company CEO or his senior designate informs the local board that someone is to be appointed. Independent directors and, for that matter, members of the subsidiary's management have been grumbling for years about this pre-emptive and even peremptory approach to CEO selection.

A far more appropriate approach and also more common, particularly today when corporate governance is in the spotlight, is for a standing board committee to have carriage of CEO succession.

The committee, working with the incumbent CEO, tracks the succession issue regularly and routinely, regardless of whether any change is imminent or not. The motto is "Stay prepared." Many factors, beyond the control of the subsidiary and beyond the likely retirement date of its CEO, come into play. For example, the current CEO may be slated for bigger things in the parent company. And of course there's always the proverbial beer truck which cuts down CEOs in their prime and necessitates a rapid and unanticipated change in leadership.

Since the board committee responsible for management succession will usually include someone from the parent organization, there will be a useful mingling of the parent's strategy and resourcing needs with those of the subsidiary. And since this will take place regularly and over a long period of time, the chances are good that a meeting of the minds will take place.

This collaborative approach is the best way to handle senior management succession in the parent-subsidiary structure where minority shareholders are involved. It is so clearly superior to the more unilateral, top-down "we've got the votes so we make the decision" approach, that I marvel that it isn't universal.

From Experience

During my service on many for-profit boards over a lot of years, I've seen as few as no CEO changes per board and as many as five. I estimate that I've observed about 60, all-in. And of those 60, perhaps 20 involved a company with a control position but with minority shareholders. And of those 20, ten or twelve were top-down and arbitrary. Often some face-saving etiquette was observed but, basically, these CEO appointments were parent-decided and parent-dictated.

Without being too specific, so as to protect the not-entirely innocent, I once sat on a board where several successive CEOs were appointed by a parent company, with only lip service given to the generally accepted view that one of a board's three highest priorities—and perhaps even its highest—is to ensure that the best possible CEO is selected.

As it happened, all parent-chosen CEOs were at least acceptable and some were superior performers. But the principle remains. A company with a regular, not an advisory, board is owed more respect by a controlling shareholder than is shown by imposing a new CEO unilaterally on that board, no matter how competent (or even, occasionally, outstanding).

In the other eight or ten cases, the process was more democratic. The subsidiary board was centrally involved. And although the parent held and expressed views, sometimes quite vigorously, its representatives were astute enough to let the board deliberate and decide.

A board with minority shareholders which is not in control of senior management succession is a board emasculated. Such a board is not much use to anyone, including the parent corporation, except as window-dressing, the listing of impressive names in an annual report. Certainly no self-respecting director should put up with no meaningful role in one of a board's two or three most central and critical responsibilities.

I should make it clear that most of the top-down approaches to CEO succession in the parent-subsidiary-minority shareholder configuration that I've observed first-hand took place before 1990. And most of the fewer cases where the board decided, not merely affirmed but actually decided, have taken place in this decade.

The culture of boards has changed massively. The boundary between what's acceptable behaviour and what's not is better defined. It has moved quite sharply to more genuine board involvement, though more remains to be done.

This movement has been assisted enormously by the much greater presence of institutional investors and by their concerns. It has also been catalysed by committees studying and recommending on how boards do and should work, committees like Dey in Canada, Cadbury and Hampel in the U.K., and the blue-ribbon panel of the National Association of Corporate Directors in the U.S.

Let me put the case even more compellingly:

- Regulatory bodies are demanding...

- Institutional investors are clamoring for...

- Committees of distinguished directors and others are recommending...

- Stock exchanges are desperately seeking...

- Individual investors are avidly hoping for...

- Pensioners are eager to see...

- The informed public is strongly supportive of...

- Corporate failures are highlighting the need for...

measures which will strengthen boards of directors so that they can and will play a more effective, consistent, diligent role. They must help to ensure that corporate performance is better, ideally much better, than it would be without them.

Widely Held Corporation

Let me turn now to the third and final kind of company, as defined by share ownership. This is the widely held corporation with no controlling shareholder. The problem of how best to choose the next CEO is obviously not complicated by the relative roles of the board and a parent company.

But another complication takes its place. And that is the relationship between board and management. Is one or the other clearly dominant? Or is there that constructive interaction between the two in which each understands and accepts a division of responsibilities in some areas and a sharing in others? In this culture, there is mutual respect between the CEO and his management team, on the one hand, and the board chairman and his fellow-directors, on the other.

The relationship is complicated by whether the CEO and the board chairman are two different persons or not. Where one person wears both hats, management is more likely to play the dominant role in CEO and senior management succession although, to be fair about it, there are exceptions.

When the board chairman is an independent director, the odds are greater that there will be a shared responsibility for CEO selection. In fact, the board and its independent directors are often the sole decision-makers. Of course, management's views and recommendations are always listened to and usually, but not always, accepted.

Ideal Scenario

Let me describe what seems to me to be close to an ideal scenario for choosing the next CEO of a widely held company. It's the process used currently in a company with which I'm familiar.

To start with, the task of CEO and senior management succession more generally rests with the Human Resource and Compensation Committee of the board. It meets about six times a year, often the day before the board meets (although the board meets more frequently). One committee meeting each year is devoted entirely to executive succession. The four outside directors on the committee, along with the CEO, review this topic thoroughly and systematically for at least two hours.

An update is provided by the CEO on his personal plans. After two or three annual iterations, it's well understood and agreed that, in some future year, perhaps give or take a year, the CEO will retire. Sometimes the date is contingent on the probability and timing of some future event or events. Sometimes it's firm.

The CEO's freedom to set his own retirement date assumes, of course, that the board is satisfied with his performance. If not, the board chooses his exit date which is likely earlier than he would prefer.

The committee spends a lot of time discussing each of the serious CEO candidates. Usually they're categorized by time-frame. Candidate A is first choice if the CEO is hit next week by that oft-cited beer truck. Candidates A, B, and C are first-tier choices if an orderly succession takes place two or three years from now. Candidates D and E, usually younger and not yet sufficiently seasoned and case-hardened, are longer-term prospects. They may be more likely to succeed the next CEO than the present one.

Lots of questions are asked:

- Are we satisfied that each candidate, especially each near-term contender, clears the minimum hurdles for CEO-ship?

- What further on-the-job training will help?

- Should lateral transfers be made to help ensure that, when the time comes, the CEO role will be filled seamlessly and with minimum disruption?

- Will additional formal training help? For example, should each of the first-tier candidates go to a finishing school like Harvard's Advanced Management Program? This needs to be scheduled well in advance, not only because demand for such programs is greater than the supply of places, but also because the three-month absence of a high-performance executive leaves a gap which must be filled judiciously.

- Are present all-in compensations competitive with the market? Are the candidates satisfied with their present status and progress? Do we know if they're getting calls from headhunters? (In the heated market for superior performers, always a scarce resource, headhunters are hyper-active. But whether the executive approached lets his CEO know is another matter.)

- Do we have adequate hooks into these stars, recognizing that signing bonuses and package buyouts are increasingly common, particularly in certain industries and when the economy is strong?

At committee meetings between one annual full-scale discussion and the next, the succession topic is always on the agenda, if only to discuss current updates. Because discussion is lively, interactive, and informal, there is an ongoing meeting of the minds on the many facets of CEO succession. Surprises are few; individual directors are comfortable with both the process and the direction which emerges from that process. So is the CEO.

When the time arrives for the CEO to retire, the decision on his replacement will be old news to the board. Consequently, succession will almost certainly be smooth and stable.

Obviously not all boards of widely held companies use such a thorough, almost textbook-perfect process. But I do believe this is likely to be the future norm. Not to belabour the obvious but ensuring that the best possible senior management and especially the best CEO are in place is one of the two or three absolutely crucial roles for a board.

I should like to end with my self-evident but nevertheless regularly disregarded mantra that a board cannot manage a company. It can, of course, dethrone a CEO and take over the leadership *temporarily*. The former CEOs of some world-class companies may still be licking the wounds they suffered from their fall from grace. But the operative word is "temporarily." Sooner or later and preferably sooner, a new CEO and perhaps even a whole new management team are appointed and the board reverts to doing what it should be doing and what it does best, namely, ensuring that there is effective management in place.

DIRECTOR RETIREMENT

The majority of Canadian public and private companies have a compulsory retirement age for directors. By far the most common arrangement is retirement if age 70 has been reached by a given annual meeting. A few industries have regulated age maximums. For example, in the insurance industry, it's 75. This usually translates into the accepted retirement age although some insurance companies have set lower limits, like 70 or 72.

The principal advantages of a predetermined retirement age are two-fold:

- It's the easy, painless, non-confrontational way to deal with directors who are no longer contributing at full potential.

- It recognizes the reality that, on average, people do slow down with age and also are more and more out of the loop as the contacts they have established over the years also age and become less active.

The principal disadvantages are these:

- A board can lose the benefit of a lifetime of accumulated experience and wisdom. While I grant that it's not the norm, there are people who are far better directors at 80 and older than some others at 40. In the Canadian setting, Allen Lambert is a classic example.[1]

- With compulsory retirement, there is a tendency to gloss over the replacement of an unsatisfactory director at an earlier age. Many chairman say to themselves with a sigh: "Time will solve this problem. We can probably tolerate a little deadwood for a while. So why should I rock the boat and create the likelihood of a situation which is likely to be embarrassing or worse?"

---

[1] For younger readers, Allen Lambert was a legendary bank CEO and is now a ledgendary director whose mental acuity has not been dulled one whit by the inevitable passage of time.

The alternative of eliminating a fixed retirement age for directors requires, indeed demands, a firm and decisive stance on replacing directors who aren't cutting it, regardless of age. The worst of all worlds is no fixed retirement age and a weak, lax policy on replacement. Inevitably, the result is boards studded with several ineffective and obsolete over-the-hillers.

On balance, the flexible approach is probably best but if and only if a director is asked to resign when his contribution at any age no longer meets the test of what's needed.[2] This requires fortitude and courage. It will, from time to time, inevitably foster ill will and even occasionally will result in litigation. Nonetheless, it's the better of two not entirely satisfactory responses to the thorny issue of director retirement.

THE BOARD OF DIRECTORS AND PENSION FUND MANAGEMENT

In the area of pension fund management, I believe that some, perhaps even many, boards of directors are under-utilized, under-informed and, therefore, at risk. There is a wide range of responses by boards to their pension fund responsibilities. I have sat on more than a dozen board committees which have some responsibility for this key function. They are called investment or finance or human resource committees. Once in a while they are even called pension committees.

---

[2] What's needed is straightforward, even simple, at the 30,000 foot level: faithful attendance, paying full attention, regular and useful contributions to discussion, taking the lead from time to time on issues, a collegial manner.

Of the dozen, several are large plans with pension fund assets of a billion dollars or more; some are medium-sized (from $50 to $150 million), and some are small (up to $40 million). Some of these plans use outside investment managers exclusively or almost exclusively. One is self-managed with respect to Canadian assets but uses an outside manager for international investments. One is totally self-managed. These two latter plans are, not surprisingly, in companies whose principal business is financial management.

In one plan, there is a board committee to examine investment performance (the asset side of pension fund management) while another committee of the same board is concerned with pension plan benefits, present and future, and actuarial liabilities (the liability side).

Based on this small sample, there is a wide range of board involvement in pension fund management. It is important to note that all of these companies once offered and some still do offer defined benefit plans where responsibility for any deficit rests squarely with the sponsoring organization. Although new plans are leaning heavily toward a defined contribution approach, the conversion of existing defined benefits plans has not been rapid.

Even with a defined contribution plan, no sponsor wants to deal with the spectre of a long-term employee about to retire with an inadequate pension due to inept investment choices. Even the question of legal liability is clouded and depends to a marked degree on several key aspects of plan implementation.

It is important to identify the major areas of pension fund sponsor responsibility so as to pinpoint the potential role of the board in these matters. On the asset management side, defined benefit plan responsibilities include:

- The decision between self-management and outside investment managers.

This is principally a function of pension fund size and economies of scale. But the decision is also influenced by the nature of the pension plan sponsor. That is, sponsors whose principal business is financial in general, investments in particular, are more likely to self-manage. The outsourcing of this function is not reassuring to their clients or potential clients.

With respect to foreign investments, a fast-growing asset for Canadian pension plans—limited in their ability to provide adequate investment diversification in the Canadian market—only a very few, very large sponsors self-manage. It's a big world out there and most Canadian pension funds invest outside Canada through alliances of various kinds with larger managers located in and closer to other economies and financial markets.

- The asset-mix decision for the pension investment portfolio.

Most pension plans tend to be conservative about the mix of equity and debt. However, it varies with where we're at in the economic cycle. For most plans, equity ranges between 30% and 70% over a full cycle.

In the long run, of course, equities outperform debt by a wide margin, probably by five to six full percentage points per annum. Unfortunately, the long run includes a few years, perhaps one or two in a decade, when equities hit the wall and are outperformed by more turtle-like debt.

And, while the long-run matters, so too does the short-run, as captured in that famous, if obvious, one-liner of John Maynard Keynes: "In the long run, we're all dead."

• The decision on the mix of balanced versus specialty managers who focus exclusively on one investment area.

Here too the decision is mostly a function of pension fund size. With funds with up to, say, $500 million of assets, balanced funds are usually more appropriate. Except for quite large pension funds, specialty managers are harder to justify. Not only is the cost higher per dollar of pension asset but there is a greater risk of spreading the assets allocated to any one class too thinly.

• The decision on the best managers to fit into this mix.

There are at least two large international organizations, Frank Russell and SEI, which earn their keep by recommending investment managers which seem best-suited for individual pension plans, each of which has its own objectives and needs.

Part of the service provided by these two firms is to rank investment managers' performance each quarter against that of their most relevant peers. This helps to weed out the more obviously unsuitable candidates although raw rankings unaccompanied by suitable context can be dangerous.

It's important to seek out enduring performance. Be wary of hot-shot funds managed (often) by high-profile individuals who get lucky for a couple of years, garnering a lot of favourable publicity in the process, but flame out over longer periods. With pension funds, remember always that it's a marathon, not a sprint.

Avoid investment manager firms where turnover is high. As a matter of fact, look for firms where turnover, excluding retirement, is non-existent. As a minimum, satisfy yourself that turnover is explained fully by reasons which do not threaten future performance. Such reasons may exist but they are uncommon in an industry which prizes continuity and stability.

- Regular investment performance review against actuarial requirements, against benchmark or benchmark-plus performance, and against performance by comparable managers.

There is a trend on the part of some actuaries to play down the comparison against other managers. But many pension committees are resisting this. It is obviously important for the portfolio to achieve internal goals, to perform as well as the broad market indices and meet or exceed actuarial requirements. But it is also important to know that each of the managers selected by the sponsor achieves at least median performance compared with other managers over a reasonable time frame, like four years. It's a competitive world out there and both absolute and relative performance need to be examined regularly.

- Lastly on the asset side, there is the responsibility to change managers from time to time as performance disappoints or occasionally unravels. Are pension plan sponsors too trigger-happy or too slow to respond? My experience suggests that, on the whole, sponsors react too slowly and therefore too late.

But I have also observed sponsors becoming slightly hysterical over a single year's performance (or even one quarter) without waiting to observe the results over a full business cycle. This seems to be particularly true with newly hired investment management firms, even though thorough due diligence was conducted prior to engagement.

On the liability side, the appropriate responsibilities include:

- The decision on overall pension plan design—including the range of benefits and any limiting conditions.

- The appointment of an actuary, usually external but occasionally in-house as with some insurance company plans.

- Regular review of the actuarial liabilities and the resulting surplus or deficit against asset values measured as required by regulators.

- The consideration and, when appropriate, approval of improvement or other changes to either the plan structure or the benefits offered.

Finally, there is plan administration, which straddles both sides of the pension fund balance sheet. The delivery system and the innumerable calculations that back it up, along with the communications that accompany it, must be both effective and efficient; otherwise the repercussions can be considerable, including the cost of reparation.

Good practice demands that the plan sponsor meet with each of the investment managers, the actuary, and the trustees regularly and routinely to discuss performance and other issues.

Returning to my original thesis, the role of the board in all of these activities is frequently insufficient to support the tenets of good corporate governance. Putting it another way, the dictates of what constitutes effective corporate governance have moved faster and more aggressively in this area, as in other areas, than companies have moved in response.

Each of the pension plan functions I have outlined obviously needs to be performed by someone. Clearly, management must continue to be the principal executor of whatever decisions are reached. What is at issue is the level of involvement of the board (and an appropriate committee of the board) in making the appropriate decisions, in monitoring ongoing performance, and in taking corrective action when necessary.

At the wrong end of the spectrum, there are companies with no board committee with pension plan responsibility. Management informs the board, probably once a year, if an actuarial surplus exists and, if so, how large. The briefing may describe overall investment results and may or may not talk about individual investment manager performance. It will likely report any changes in managers during the past year, and, although this is less likely, might even mention asset mix.

All this is reported after the fact, except in egregious cases of clear and evident mismanagement. In general, the input of the board is not sought.

At the other end of this spectrum, a pension committee of the board is charged with a well-defined and well-documented responsibility for overseeing all aspects of the company's pension plan.

This committee meets between four and six times a year. It interacts with each manager at least once a year, often twice with managers with problems. It meets with an independent performance evaluation firm once a quarter to discuss both summary and component performance of the pension portfolio.

It determines the most appropriate asset mix for the plan in total and approves asset mix changes requested by individual balanced fund managers. It determines when a plan is large enough to move to specialty management. It decides on the number of managers and which mandate should be given to which manager.

The same spectrum of board involvement can be found on the liability side, varying between the most desultory kind of after-the-fact communication to approval of all of the important steps in the sequence of pension plan design.

There are a number of reasons commonly cited for not involving boards in pension fund management. One is that directors have neither the expertise to contribute usefully nor the time to acquire the expertise. If this argument is to carry any weight at all, it should apply to almost every aspect of corporate governance. In which case, the board is largely redundant except as a legal necessity and a rubber stamp. Obviously, this flies in the face of contemporary corporate governance.

Furthermore, most directors do their homework, are reasonably quick studies, and, through experience, have learned to ask perceptive questions even in areas where they are not highly experienced and have less than complete knowledge. There is almost no topic so esoteric that it cannot be reduced, via clear presentation and communication, into a few reasonably well-defined issues requiring decisions.

I have heard it said that some external investment managers would prefer to deal primarily, if not exclusively, with inside management. No doubt it complicates things to bring a board committee of outside directors into the equation. It represents still another set of influences for advisors to deal with. But advisors are well paid to deal with layers of complexity and even, at times, ambiguity.

Finally, there is the sad fact that a few, only a few, fortunately, senior managements from the Mesozoic Era continue to want to keep their boards out of their pockets (or is it in their pockets?) and want to control them by that once-popular stratagem known colloquially as the mushroom theory. But, to state the obvious, the world of business is changing; managements who resist the tide of greater accountability for chief executive officers and other senior executives are, to continue the metaphor, likely to be swept out to sea.

Some Personal Experiences as a Director (II)

In 1984, Gordon Gray and I negotiated the sale of control of what was then A.E. LePage to Brascan/Trilon/Royal Trust. Prior to the sale, 87% of the shares were held by the people who worked there. After the sale, this dropped to 47%. The name of the company was changed to Royal LePage (which struck most of us as a plus, something akin to "By Appointment to Her Majesty").

Gordon and I were each directors of companies which competed with some part of the Brascan group. In my case, there were two such companies. One was Costain, a property developer. The other was General Accident Assurance, a property and casualty insurance company. Costain competed with Trizec; General Accident competed with

Wellington Insurance, a subsidiary of London Life. Gordon faced similar conflicts. As part of the merger negotiations, we each agreed to resign from the boards of all competing companies.

A year or so later, I joined the boards of Trizec and of London Life. Parenthetically and somewhat ironically, the Brascan group later sold Trizec to Peter Munk's Horsham Corporation and sold Wellington to the Ing Group of the Netherlands. Even more ironically, Costain was itself later sold to Brascan; the name was changed to Coscan and the company was eventually merged into Brascan's Brookfield Properties. London Life was sold much later—in 1997—to Great West Life after an earlier and lower bid by the Royal Bank.

And what are the governance lessons in all of this? The important one is that conflicts of interest need to be dealt with and resolved. It's a cop-out to say "Everyone has conflicts; they simply have to be managed." Not good enough, not anymore. In an age in which the media are pervasive and powerful, perception is at least as important as reality. And the perception of conflict is enough to bring serious criticism to those involved, no matter how much they "manage" that conflict with probity and discretion.

Now on to my second story. For nearly three years in the mid-90's, I served as board chairman of a newly-formed company named Primaris Corporate Services. Primaris was and is a property and asset manager and a real estate advisor to Canadian companies like IBM. The company was formed as a 50-50 joint venture between Trizec (later Trizec Hahn) and a subsidiary of the Texas-based development company, Trammell Crow. Each of these two owners was and is a large, successful, proud, aggressive corporation.

My role was to act as a neutral, non-executive chairman. Since I was no longer on the Trizec board after Brascan sold it to Horsham, I did not face any conflict. Unfortunately, the level of institutional wariness between the Trizec and Trammell Crow board members (two from each organization) was high from the outset and it never really dissipated. Think of it as a more civilized, modern-day version of the Montagues and the Capulets.

After less than three years, one of the two partners pulled the trigger of the shotgun arrangement which had been built into the original agreement between the two companies. As a result, in 1996 Trammell Crow bought out Trizec's 50% ownership of Primaris and operated it as a wholly owned subsidiary.

There are two lessons here. The first is that a neutral chairman needs to be hyper-sensitive to the nuances and the early warning signals. I needed to bring the two sides together more frequently and informally than only at board meetings. Franker and fuller discussion from the outset might have allowed this uneasy alliance to survive.

Which leads me to a closely related second lesson. At the time of my involvement with Primaris, I was sitting on a dozen and a half other boards and chairing four or five of them. I was also devoting a day a week to the chairmanship of the board of York University.

I mention this, not as an excuse but as an object-lesson. You do no favours to anyone, including yourself, by getting overextended. Easy to say; harder to do. Nevertheless, experience has taught me that a CEO should never take on more than two outside boards and a full-time director (which, by 1993, I was) should limit his or her boards to some number. And what is that number? While it probably should vary from person to person, I do believe that, in today's demanding environment, the upper limit is definitely a number with only one digit.

It's clear that boards today require far more time, effort, and commitment than ever before, more than even a decade ago. And it's up to each of us who accept directorships to say "no" more frequently than some of us do.

Finally, let me describe a more recent situation involving a Canadian investment management firm called Perigee. Operating principally in the field of pension fund management, secondarily with high net worth individuals and in a smaller way with mutual funds, Perigee had over 21 billion dollars of assets under management by mid-2000.

In 1998, Perigee went public, doing a secondary offering of 30% of its shares and listing them on the TSE. Several months earlier, a board had been assembled in preparation for public-company status. It consisted of three management representatives, including the company's CEO, Alex Wilson; two representatives of Clarica (which held just under 20% of the shares), including its CEO, Bob Astley; and six independents. I was asked to chair the board and I accepted.

In the two years after it went public, the company's performance was excellent in terms of revenue growth, earnings growth, and level of profitability. However, the share price, issued at $20, went briefly to as high as $23 but then slowly drifted down to as low as $15 in the early part of 2000.

Over these same two years, the board and management discussed at length various strategic alternatives available to the company. Eventually it became clear that the preferred option was to partner with or sell to a large, reputable U.S. firm in the same line of business. The reasons, all loosely connected, included these:

- The lacklustre performance of Canadian versus U.S. and some other foreign equities over more than a decade, excepting only a short period in the recent past, has created a strong demand by Canadians to invest more of their money outside Canada.

- The limitations on registered pension funds owning foreign securities are less than they were and will likely be still less than now proclaimed. Furthermore, the use of derivative funds abrogates the problem altogether.

- Finally, a cheap Canadian dollar makes an acquisition attractive to both a foreign buyer and a Canadian seller of companies.

In May of 2000, for these and other reasons, the shareholders approved a recommendation, supported by the board and management and the investment bankers selected to produce a fairness opinion, to sell 100% of Perigee shares to Legg Mason of Baltimore in exchange for a tranche of their shares. Legg Mason is a highly respected, 103-year old company which offers as its mission statement, this succinct one-liner: "A global financial services company with one product: advice."

There are, I think, two lessons in this case, one for directors and one for public policy-makers. For directors, it demonstrates still another time that one can never assume that the status quo will last for long. That is, it is increasingly unlikely that the future will be like the present.

For policy-makers, the lesson is that not even the most-profitable, best-managed, most-respected Canadian corporations in any field will survive, let alone thrive, unless the macro-environment is and remains supportive. In some industries—including the management of other people's money—the problem is more acute than in others. An anaemic Canadian dollar does not help.

PART 3

The Fine Print:
Compensation and Accreditation

CHAPTER 8

Compensation of Company Directors

A certain amount of sound and fury is being generated in the U.S. these days on the subject of director compensation.

Criticism is directed primarily to three areas:

1. Some companies pay what is perceived to be an excessive amount of cash compensation.

2. Perks such as pension plans for directors and charitable donations made on behalf of directors should be eliminated.

3. There should be a greater emphasis on share ownership.

Graef Crystal, a U.S. corporate-compensation expert, has developed a matrix which measures company size and performance against director compensation and which produces a list of what he calls "black hats" and "white hats." These are companies where directors are either overpaid or underpaid to a marked degree.

For example, Bausch & Lomb paid its directors in 1994 an average of $139,000 (U.S.); his model of pay for performance and size says they should have been paid $47,700 per year. By contrast, Alcan Aluminum, a Canadian company which lists its shares on the NYSE, paid its directors $25,000 (U.S.) per year; his model say they should have been paid $63,000 per year.

The Bausch & Lomb numbers pale in comparison with some later ones. In 1998, a mere four years later, eighteen public companies in the U.S. paid each of their directors in excess of $250,000 U.S., including options. The highest five paid from $551,000 (Sun Microsystems; how the mighty have fallen!) to $684,000 (Cisco Systems; ditto).

The lowest paid board, by contrast, was that of Berkshire Hathaway at $14,400, but more than worth it for the privilege of rubbing shoulders and trading pithy comments with Warren Buffett, arguably the greatest value investor of all time.

Now let's broaden the discussion to compare Canadian and U.S. directors' fees. Various studies yield somewhat different results but a rough average comparison, across a wide range of industries and company sizes, shows that directors of Canadian companies were paid $22,000 (Cdn.) of total cash compensation in 1999. The comparable number for directors of U.S. companies was $62,000 (U.S.). This is obviously a very great difference which is much larger again if the comparison is made in a common currency. At the date of this writing, $1.00 (U.S.) is worth $1.60 (Cdn.).

However, studies which have attempted to adjust for company size and profitability produce a rather more reasonable comparison. A William Mercer study compared Canadian and U.S. companies with revenues in the 1.4 to 1.5 billion dollars (Cdn.) range. This showed that the annual retainer was $15.3K (Cdn.) for Canadian directors and $31.7K (U.S.) for U.S. directors. The total cash comparison was $40.8K (Can.) to $51.2K (U.S.) and the total direct comparison (including the present value of options) was $87.2K (Cdn.) to $98.1K (U.S.).

Although the attempt to compare apples and apples reduces the differences to somewhat more reasonable levels, they continue to be significant. Some U.S. directors may well be overpaid but it is quite clear that most Canadian directors are still, on average, almost certainly underpaid. The old saying that a Canadian director is the best bargain in town may not be quite as true as it was ten or fifteen years ago, but it is not much of an exaggeration either.

Later I'll discuss how much and how Canadian directors should be paid. But first I should like to focus on three aspects of director compensation.

First is the issue of share ownership by directors. We should distinguish between shares purchased by a director with his own funds and share ownership as an integral part of director compensation. On the former, I'm opposed to mandatory share ownership requirements. Voluntary ownership is obviously desirable but mandatory share ownership involving a significant dollar investment forces directors into decisions which may be financially imprudent (depending on the economic cycle, the state of direction of industry and/or company performance, and other considerations). This does not refer to ownership of, say, 100 shares, which is merely a nominal concession to a principle.

Share ownership as a component of directors' compensation is quite a different matter. It is growing in importance and it should be encouraged. More details about this later.

On the issue of stock grants versus stock options, I favour some of each. With options, more leverage and, therefore, a greater incentive can be granted per present-value dollar of compensation, since only future share appreciation counts, as measured by the Black-Scholes or other model.

A criticism sometimes levelled at options is that directors have only the upside and none of the downside, while shareholders who have purchased their shares have both. This criticism is misdirected. If the price of a director's stock does not go up, he forgoes compensation for services rendered. Putting it another way, he "paid for" his options at the time they were granted, so long as the value of those options was included in the mix of components adding up to all-in competitive compensation. The "so long as" condition is, of course, key.

If options are used, I believe the following ground rules are desirable:

- They should be granted at market price. In any event, accounting rules militate against options issued at below-market strike prices.

- Their value should be an integral component of planned compensation, all-in. This may seem obvious but I have occasionally seen cases where option grants have been handled almost as an afterthought and yet where the eventual financial reward dwarfed the other components of director compensation.

- The sale of shares through the exercise of options should generally be minimized, except in unusual circumstances. Certainly some shares acquired should be held until a director retires or resigns. A former exception was the sale of enough shares to pay capital gain tax but recent changes in tax law (no tax until the shares are sold) make this unnecessary.

The second area on which I'd like to comment is the choice between an annual retainer and an annual retainer plus a meeting fee. Each approach has its pluses and minuses. An annual retainer alone is clear and simple to administer. It facilitates calling frequent, short telephonic board meetings without concern about whether and how much directors should be paid. Some telephonic meetings last 15 or 20 minutes and sometimes even less if the sole purpose of the meeting is to ratify a previously discussed, straightforward decision.

On the other hand, attendance at board meetings does matter and incentives to encourage attendance can help. While almost all directors are both conscientious and conscious of their obligations, scheduling conflicts and consequent determination of priorities do exist.

I rather like what might be called the "modified tontine"[1] approach. For each board or board committee meeting, a pot is created by multiplying the per-meeting fee by the number of paid directors eligible to attend. The pot is then divided among the paid directors in attendance. This may be a touch esoteric for wide-spread use but it certainly underscores the importance of being there.

Finally, let me say a few words about the process for setting directors' compensation. The most common approach is for this matter to be determined by a board committee. Sometimes it is a compensation committee; sometimes a corporate governance committee, which is growing in popularity; sometimes an executive committee, which is declining in popularity.

The only problem with any of these committees is that they're almost invariably dominated by outside directors. Directors, like any other constituency in society, should not set their own compensation. This was less important when director compensation was small enough in aggregate that it didn't create enough self-interest to be a problem.

This was especially so when most corporate board members were CEOs and other senior executives, either active or recently retired, and where director compensation constituted a small part of their total income.

It is more important today when director compensation has grown appreciably from, say, a decade ago and when stock options have paid off handsomely for many directors. Furthermore, directors today are drawn, at least

---

[1] A tontine is a winner-take-all agreement in which the last living party to that agreement is the sole winner.

in a limited way, from a broader universe than only better-paid members of society, such as senior executives.

I should add that self-interest is, in practice, at least on boards with which I'm familiar, not much of an issue. Nevertheless, even the possibility of self-interest, coupled with a growing comprehension that perception is reality, suggests that there are better ways to deal with director compensation.

A second approach is for management to bring recommendations to the full board for approval. To the extent that self-interest is a problem with the first approach, it's a problem with this one as well. And again, at least according to the tenets of governance theory, it sets up a potentially unhealthy mutual interdependence between the board and management. After all, the board or a committee of the board sets management compensation, at least in public companies without a controlling shareholder.

A third approach is to use a reputable compensation consultant. This has merit so long as the consultant does not benefit significantly from other company assignments. There may in fact be a useful role for an independent specialized consultant who focuses exclusively on this narrow mandate.

Now on to the always interesting questions of how much Canadian directors should be paid and what is the best mix of the components of directors' compensation.

In response to the first question, there are various relevant comparators.

1. What are directors being paid in Canada?

2. What are they being paid in the U.S.? As Canada and the U.S. have been drawn inexorably closer together,

economically, culturally, and in every other significant way[2], the only comparison which matters to Canadian directors (and executives and indeed wage-earners more generally) is with the U.S.

3. How much time do directors spend on board business over a year?

4. What does the CEO earn?

5. What do the higher-paid directors on the board earn in their "day jobs"?

The first and second queries were addressed earlier in this article. Across a wide range of industries and company sizes, Canadian directors were paid in 1999 an average of $22,000 Canadian while U.S. directors were paid an average of about $62,000 U.S.

Unfortunately, this comparison does not adjust for:

• company size

• whether the company is a wholly owned subsidiary, is a company controlled by a single shareholder but with a public float, or is widely held

• industry segment

• level of profitability

• a common currency

---

[2] We may persist in pronouncing the occasional word differently, like *roof* or *about*, and in spelling words like *humour* and *valour* and *sceptre* and *mitre* differently as residual tribute to our British history and heritage. Such superficial and increasingly quaint distinctions help us to ignore comfortably the profound integrative and assimilative changes which have been going on since the end of WWII.

On average, Canadian companies are smaller, less profitable, less likely to be widely held, and more likely to be in one of the resource or service sectors.

I am not aware of any study which eliminates all of these apple and orange factors. But the Mercer study mentioned earlier in this chapter found that, after adjusting for revenue differences—admittedly, with a fairly small sample (companies with annual revenues in the range of 1.4 to 1.5 million Canadian dollars)—total cash compensation in a common currency was in the ratio 1 to 2. This is greater by an appreciable margin than all-in productivity comparisons between Canada and the U.S.

Now let's come at this matter of appropriate director compensation from a quite different perspective. Let's examine how much time a director spends on his duties in a year and taking into account the greater demands placed on him in this evolved environment where governance matters and is taken seriously. Obviously there's no single answer. The variation we find is magnified by the fact that we're in a period of a major change in expectations of directors; some companies have adjusted for this much earlier and faster than others.

Based on various surveys as well as on personal experience and that of other directors with whom I've discussed this matter, the range of time requirements might be something like this:

	The Low-End Case	The High-End Case
• Number of board meetings per year	4	12
• Number of board committee memberships per average director	1	2
• Number of meetings per average board committee per year.	1	5
• Average meeting length in hours	2	4.5
• Average preparation time per meeting in hours	2	4.5
• Travel time in hours per meeting per average director (assume no separate trip for committee meetings)	2	2
• Total hours required per year per director	28	222

As we move from the low-end to the high-end case, the data become less descriptive, more normative. Obviously the low-end estimate applies to a board which hasn't yet begun to adapt to contemporary demands. The high-end estimate is still unusual, even today, but it does provide a glimpse of the near future if corporate governance continues to evolve in the direction in which it is currently heading.

To convert hours to dollars requires us to value a director's time. Two relevant measures are a company's CEO's compensation and the opportunity cost of the higher-paid directors on a given board.

Assume that a typical Canadian CEO works, on average, 3,000 hours per year and that he earns (on average), all-in, between $500,000 and $2,000,000 per year. This includes salary, bonus, stock options, pension plan, and other benefits. This range includes the great majority of CEOS of companies above a minimum size cut-off. It results in a minimum per-hour compensation of $167 and a maximum of $667.

Since the higher-paid directors on any given board will typically be the CEOs of other companies of comparable size, the earnings calculation is the same. Senior partners of large law firms earn somewhat above the middle of this range.

Converting hours to dollars, we obtain a very wide range of appropriate Canadian director compensation: from about $4,700 per year all the way up to $148,000. By applying the time requirements of a given board, a specific annual compensation number can be calculated. For the most part, it will be considerably higher than current practice.

It reflects what a director should be paid if he responds in full measure to what is expected, indeed demanded, in an increasingly litigious, complex, and challenging society.

Turning now to compensation mix, the components normally used include:

- per-annum fees

- per-meeting fees

- stock option or stock grants (often on a tax-deferred basis, i.e., deferred stock units or DSUs).[3]

---

3 Deferred stock units are vehicles through which the transfer of share ownership and, as a consequence, related tax obligations for the director-shareholder are deferred into the future, often until retirement.

- Other, such as pension arrangements, life insurance, donation benefits, etc.

I exclude bonuses, as do virtually all companies, because they're normally awarded for short-term performance. Directors should take a longer-term view. For the most part, that's where their influence is felt most.

I also exclude the category "other." In Canada, these "extras" are uncommon; in the U.S., they have been more common but are becoming much less so as institutional shareholders and others attack them as gratuitous add-ons.

Despite the fact that the Cadbury Report in the U.K. did not regard options for directors as good practice, most U.S. and many Canadian companies have already included options as an integral part of director compensation. As discussed earlier, I prefer options to grants for two reasons: more bang for the buck and more tax-effective. Using both may be the best of all worlds.

A few other points follow:

- Cash retainer fees should constitute between one-third and one-half of total compensation.

- The remaining one-half to two-thirds should be divided between stock grants and stock options.

- Stock grants will normally be made annually. They should be made at the same time each year, such as five days after the date of the annual meeting. This eliminates the possibility of any charge of self-dealing.

- Stock options will be issued at market price and, though they can be granted annually, it is simpler and more common to grant them less frequently, like every three years. Regardless of frequency, option grants, like stock grants, should be made at the same time of year.

• The proportion of stock grants to options will vary from company to company. For reasons already stated, I prefer a higher weighting to options.

Director
Accreditation

After thinking about the matter for some time, I wrote
an article in 1998 on the subject of director accreditation.
I tried to examine the issue objectively and without prejudice and I concluded, tentatively, that this is an idea
whose time, if it has not yet come, is probably approaching. In the United Kingdom, director accreditation (or certification) was adopted a few years ago under the auspices
of the Institute of Directors (IOD). Britain became the first
developed country to move solidly in this direction.

And while the mix of inside to outside directors is much
higher in the U.K. than in Canada or the U.S., the principle
of fostering a better-trained and, therefore, better-prepared
director class is universal.

What does accreditation involve? Its components would include a pre-test educational program, an entry-level test, an appropriate designation for those who both passed the test and had at least three years' experience on the board of a publicly listed company, and continuing education. An appropriate disciplinary process would be put in place to help maintain professional standards and deal with serious infractions. All of which would require a small, permanent secretariat to be paid for through annual membership fees.

A first draft of my article was circulated to a dozen and a half experienced and well-known directors with views on this topic and whose judgement I respect. This evoked a wide range of relevant insights, persuading me to do a substantial redraft. It was then published in Canada in the *Ivey Business Quarterly* (Winter 1998-1999 issue), and in the U.S. in *The Corporate Board: The Leading Journal of Corporate Governance* (January/February 1999 issue). Subsequently, it appeared in the August 2000 issue of *Director's Monthly*, the official newsletter of the National Association of Corporate Directors in the U.S.

In the *Ivey Business Quarterly*, it was accompanied by a reasoned rebuttal by Professor Don Thain and by short excerpts from letters and phone calls from some of those to whom I had sent the first draft. Appendix A on page 215 contains the full text of the Ivey article and excerpts from the views of several of my correspondents.

Based on responses to my article to date as well as on many discussions with other directors, CEOs, and associates from various fields, there is considerable support for the concept in some circles but scepticism in others.

At the risk of overgeneralization, those generally in favour are members of other professions, institutional investors, facilitators and intermediaries in the buying and selling of securities, persons with regulatory responsibilities, providers of liability insurance, and some directors. Those generally opposed or at least wary are CEOs and other senior executives, some academics, and some directors.

As just noted, directors tend to be divided. Those who are also CEOs and those who are older and have sat on boards for years run the gamut from doubtful through leery to opposed. Other directors tend to be more supportive, depending, of course, on the specifics.

One important specific is whether accreditation is voluntary or mandatory. It is very clear that support for the principle is based on a voluntary model. Compulsory accreditation is supported by almost no one (although some view it as a possible subsequent step, should the voluntary model prove over time to be widely accepted and highly successful).

Those who expressed qualms about accreditation, even on a voluntary basis, used arguments like these[1] and others listed in my article:

- "Directorship is not a profession any more than being a CEO is a profession. We don't accredit CEOs; they earn their spurs by performance on the job."

- "It is demeaning to think of directors in terms of licensing—for that's what accreditation or certification is a euphemism for. Many directors, usually senior members

---

[1] Some of these five points are direct quotes; some have been paraphrased.

of the business community and often of society more broadly, will find this sort of regimentation and conformity too binding, even offensive."

• "Even a director accreditation process operated entirely within the private sector would be only a step removed from government intervention and even control. It might tempt government at some level to get involved or even to take over the process."

• "There are already enough uncertainties, difficulties and pitfalls with being a director today. The all-in reward/ risk profile is not particularly attractive. The compensation per hour is less, sometimes considerably less, than that earned by CEOs or senior legal counsel or investment bankers. By superimposing another stratum of complication, the net calculus of directorship deteriorates further."

• "And as a friend recently said to me, 'I don't want to sit on ten boards and become a so-called professional director. As CEO of a public company, I just want to sit on my own board without having to go through a rigamarole of unnecessary complications. Is that too much to ask?'"

Some of these and other concerns are directed more at mandatory than at voluntary accreditation, but the remote possibility that one could lead to the other may explain why even the principle is viewed with some agnosticism.

On the other side of the ledger, the central argument supporting voluntary accreditation is a belief, partly reasoned and partly intuitive, that corporate performance would, on average and over time, be enhanced. This assumes, of course, that good directorship matters. If it doesn't, the entire concept of corporate governance is a mockery.

The crux of the matter is whether corporate performance is likely to be improved by directors who are better-trained, who agree to stay current on rapidly evolving changes in the business environment and in what constitutes good, contemporary directorship, and who accept the sorts of disciplines normal in most professions. While there is no way to know for certain, there is, I believe, a growing conviction among reasonable and informed men and women that it will. After careful consideration of the upsides and the downsides and after consequent ambivalence, I have come to believe this as well. (See Appendix A for more on this issue.)

Executive Compensation Issues

Over the past several years, there have been expressed in various circles considerable anguish and teeth-gnashing over senior executive compensation levels. Most of this criticism both arises in and is directed at the U.S., where compensation is highest (and where stock markets were exuberantly bullish for longest).

The criticism varies with its source but includes these concerns:

- There is a widening, yawning gap between the compensation of CEOs and "working stiffs."

- In too many companies, all-in compensation at the top has reached obscene (this adjective is used routinely) levels.

- There is or there is perceived to be an inadequate linkage between pay and performance.
- There are concerns about some aspects of the process for determining senior executive compensation.

Let me begin with a miscellany of facts and opinions from a variety of sources, some hostile, some not. I'll focus on the U.S. because of the abundance of data and because they lead the parade. And where they lead, other members of the developed world, like Canada, often follow with a lag period that continues to grow shorter.

FACT: A recent survey by William Mercer found that the median compensation in 1998 of the CEOs of 350 large U.S. companies was $8.6 million. (This and all dollar figures in this article are in U.S. currency.)

FACT: In 1998, Mel Karmazin, CBS Chairman, earned $200 million. Salary and bonus came to $9.8 million; the rest was option gains.

FACT: *The Economist* has reported that CEO compensation in ten large companies, selected for comparability, in each of the U.S. and the U.K., showed the following for 1998:

	Salary Plus Bonus ($ millions)	Unrealized Option Gains ($ millions)
U.K.	1.60	13.46
U.S.	4.34	76.00
Ratio of U.K. to U.S.	.37	.18

Comparable data for Canada suggests that Canadian CEOs, comparing apples to apples as best we can, are somewhat higher than U.K. levels but very much closer to them than to U.S. levels.

FACT: Brian Hall of Harvard Business School recently quantified the fact that options constitute by far the largest part of U.S. senior executive pay which is "performance-related." His quote marks imply at least some doubts about the performance aspects of high price-earnings multiples in raging bull markets. Or as the head of the U.K.'s largest pension fund manager, Hermes, is quoted as saying, "Never confuse a bull market with genius."

Hall's calculations show that, for any given increase in the price of a company's shares, the increase in the value of stocks and stock options held by the CEOs of a large sample of U.S. companies was 53 times the increase in the sum of salary and bonus.

FACT: Graef Crystal, long an implacable critic of excessive and unjustified compensation levels, said recently that, in 1998, a large-company CEO in the U.S. was paid 350 times as much as the average worker. By 1999, this ratio had increased to 575. The comparable ratio in Japan is less than 10, though Japan is not necessarily the best exemplar these days.

Crystal went on to make an inflammatory and apocalyptic prediction: "In 2010, the gap will be like that of the one between Louis XVI and his workers—and you know what happened to Louis XVI."

FACT: On April 29, 1999, the *Wall Street Journal* published an article with this subheading: "U.S. companies find creative ways to ensure executive pay keeps pace with bull markets."

The article cited the increasing prevalence of special bonuses, over and above regular compensation, for things like reducing losses, successful completion of divestitures, completing an acquisition when "other suitors were vying for it," and, for a CEO approaching retirement, "implementing a smooth transition of his responsibilities."

The article wondered, somewhat plaintively, whether these sorts of activities aren't what CEOs are paid to do in the first place. In 1998, 9% of S&P 500 companies awarded these special bonuses, often justifying them, perhaps a little guiltily, on the grounds that they were necessary to prevent a valued CEO from jumping ship.

FACT: A year earlier, in its April 9, 1998 edition, the same *WSJ* published a special supplement on executive pay. The first two paragraphs of a series of articles over eighteen broadsheet pages set the tone:

"Gilbert F. Amelio cried all the way to the bank. During his 17-month tenure as head of Apple Computer Inc., the company racked up losses totalling nearly $2 billion. But when the board ousted him last summer, Mr. Amelio walked away with severance pay of $6.7 million, in addition to his $2 million in salary and bonus for the year ended September 26. Mr. Amelio vows to seek a still juicier deal in his next CEO job. Despite the severance windfall, he says the Apple package "didn't protect my downside as well as I had hoped it would." Welcome aboard the Chief Executive Gravy Train. It overflows with treasure when things go well—and even when they don't. ...For top corporate bosses, the message seems to be: No gain, little pain."

In the same supplement, the *Journal* described a Web site on executive pay sponsored by the AFL-ClO. Some of the responses were predictably incendiary: "It seems that *Fortune 500* executives are poor students of history. Have they never heard of liberté, égalité, fraternité? They must be begging for guillotine."

All these ominous references to the French Revolution are, of course, more than a little overwrought but they illustrate a mindset that's out there.

FACT: In 1996, Jack Welch, GE's then Chairman and CEO, earned $27.6 million, all-in. But there's a but. Over his then seventeen years at the helm, the market value of GE's shares increased by over $225 billion.

So much for an anecdotal sampling of fact and opinion. The pertinent questions which flow from these include:

• Is all of this nothing more than evidence that the market is working? Does it simply reflect the market interaction of two basic truths: there is a burgeoning demand for leaders who can run successfully enterprises as large as some countries and there is an acute scarcity of persons who can do it?

- If we are dealing with a market issue, is it a free, well-functioning market or is it skewed in one or more ways in favour of rapidly increasing and unwarranted compensation levels?

- To the extent that the solution is to link compensation more closely with performance, a point on which most observers agree, is the relationship good enough? If performance is defined as share prices moving up because the public capitalizes earnings at ever higher multiples (at least partly because the baby boom generation, as it proceeds through its savings phase, is sustaining such multiples), the answer is no, the relationship is not good enough.

  Even rewards based on peer group comparisons fall prey to the same flaw. Surely it's better to link performance and pay (through options, as now) but restrict exercise until some stretch but attainable improvement in absolute company performance is achieved, as measured by such variables as ROI, ROE, or EPS. Performance options then mean what they say.

- Finally, is this issue of executive pay entirely an economic issue, that is, balancing the supply of and demand for talent in a surging economy extending over more than eight years?[1] Or is there any moral/ethical/social/community issue here?

Let's consider each of these questions in turn. To repeat, are today's compensation levels simply evidence that a market is working? Is it merely the interaction of an enormous demand for exceptional business leaders with the evident reality that they are a scarce resource?

---

[1] In early 2000, the surging economy ceased temporarily to surge. But the wheel will, as always, turn again and perhaps sooner than later.

If so, why should we be surprised that senior executive compensation levels have risen so dramatically? After all, top athletes, rock stars, movie stars and TV personalities earn at least as much as top corporate executives. The career earnings of Madonna and Michael Eisner are probably in the same ballpark.

Ignoring the fact that few business leaders earn anything from the lucrative business of testimonials, is there a difference in the process by which the compensation of a great athlete and a great corporate leader is determined?

Consider Michael Jordan. In his case, the concept of a market seemed to work pretty well. His worth was based on his individual achievements from which his audience appeal flowed. A host of statistics on his performance were scrutinized meticulously by many.

By contrast, the compensation of Jack Welch was predicated on his performance as the leader of a vast organization. Most of the statistics, equally well scrutinized, though by a different crowd, relate to the corporation which he led rather than to him as an individual.

Perhaps the market for an individual performer is purer and more transparent and more comprehensible than for a corporate leader. However, this certainly does not imply that the value to society of a highly effective leader of a corporation with enormous economic impact is less than that of a great tenor, third baseman, or actor blessed with highly appealing physical attributes. Microsoft's market capitalization in 2000 was larger than the GNP of all but eight countries.

What it does imply is that the market value of an individual performing primarily as an individual is easier to evaluate and price than that of an individual leading an organization. To illustrate, how much does the power of a household name brand, like Coca-Cola, which has been around for well over a century, contribute to corporate performance? Or what is the value of a basic patent which, through extensions, has contributed overwhelmingly to somebody's bottom line for thirty years? Such legacies predate current CEOs but obviously benefit current performance.

All of which suggests that, to the greatest extent possible, the market price of corporate leaders not be further complicated or skewed by faulty process. Fortunately, some of the traditional and well-publicized ways of introducing bias are less prevalent today as corporate governance practices, under intense public scrutiny, have improved.

For example, it was once not uncommon for CEOs to sit on each other's boards and to sit on or even chair each other's compensation committees. Today, that's anathema. Similarly, for a supplier (like a company's outside legal counsel or investment banker) to sit on or chair a board compensation committee is unlikely these days.

The potential for conflict in these circumstances is both palpable and considerable. A short but classic anecdote illustrates the point. The players shall remain nameless if only because, when last I checked, a four-year-old shareholder's suit was still wandering through a legal labyrinth.

About a decade ago, the CEO of a large U.S. manufacturing company and the CEO of a large U.S. commercial bank sat on each other's boards and eventually chaired each other's board compensation committees. They had been good friends for years, playing quite a lot of golf together and seeing each other, with their wives, socially.

As it happened, the two compensation committee chair appointments were within a few months of being contemporaneous. At the time, both men, in their day jobs, were at or close to the median of peer-group comparisons, all-in.

Three and a half years later, each had managed to claw his way up the pay ladder to first-quartile compensation levels, despite the shareholder suit allegation that corporate performance was (how to put this diplomatically?) abysmal in one company and lousy in the other.

I realize that such a blatant example of feather-bedding is atypical but I confess that, when I first heard about this sorry tale, my scepticism and perhaps even cynicism about any governance regime which tolerated such incestuous goings-on rose to new highs.

More broadly, the majority of companies, reacting to widespread criticism, are trying to tie executive compensation more tightly, more rigorously, to performance. And performance is increasingly, though anything but universally, defined as something more than a company's share price rising in tandem with stock market indexes generally. When a rising tide lifts all boats, the argument for exceptional compensation demands that performance also be genuinely exceptional.

But there are more deeply ingrained practices which continue to distort executive compensation upwards. Compensation consultants are usually hired by managements and they know who pays their rent. I am not suggesting improbity or reckless disregard for the truth. But comparative compensation data are subject to interpretation which is sometimes skewed a little by mutual self-interest. Also, judgements on performance often include a qualitative and subjective component. And beauty is in the eye of the beholder.

In addition, the board is often the captive of management, even today. This is least likely with companies where there is a control block. Directors representing that block usually exert a strong moderating influence. It is most likely in a widely held company where the roles of the board chairman and CEO are combined and in which many of the directors were appointed by that chairman/CEO and owe him some measure of loyalty and allegiance. Also, CEOs sitting on a board bring a perspective to the table similar to that of the incumbent CEO and are sympathetic to compensation aspirations.

Based on a fair amount of hands-on experience, it's clear to me that the process for determining senior compensation levels varies widely from company to company. It ranges from 99 44/100% pure through modestly skewed to shamelessly rigged.

But even a little bias is contagious. That is, if your competitor's processes are skewed to greater compensation growth than warranted by performance, it's difficult for your company to ignore this. It puts at risk your ability to retain your key people. As that well-known monetary generalization puts it, "Bad money drives out good." This might be translated, when discussing compensation, into "More money drives out less." Mandatory disclosure of senior executive compensation almost certainly compounds the problem, despite the hopes and expectations of those who sponsored the requisite regulations.

The final question I want to address is whether excessive executive pay levels have broader, societal implications which transcend the narrower though important question of whether or not the shareholder is well-served.

Many years ago, at a time when oil was thought to be a rapidly declining resource, I attended a lecture at a university by a very senior member of the oil business. During the Q & A that followed, a student chided the speaker for having been driven to the lecture in a gas-guzzling limousine, reminding him of his eloquent remarks on the virtues of conservation. To which the speaker replied with considerable sang froid, "Whoever said life is fair?"

I have often thought about this riposte. In one sense, that executive, a man whom I knew and respected, was merely giving voice to the obvious: that the lexicon of economics does not include concepts of fairness or unfairness. Except for a few economic philosophers like J.K. Galbraith, the world's leading economists, including almost all of the profession's Nobel Laureates, worry about effectiveness and efficiency, not about concepts as elusive and, well, uneconomic as justice and fairness.

As I noted earlier, in 1998 a typical large company CEO was paid 350 times as much as the average American worker. By 1999, this disparity had risen to 575 times. This probably wouldn't have surprised those mediaeval philosophers who debated at length the concept of a just wage. After all, a 14th-century king and serf would have produced even more extreme comparisons. But that was then and this is now. Democracies tolerate inequities less well than absolute monarchies.

In this wider context, two comments seem relevant to any discussion of contemporary executive compensation. The first is that, while only a misanthrope or one infected by schadenfreude would wish for a market meltdown and/or a recession, even an optimist might predict this. It's a safe bet that even the most stable and successful national economies are more cyclical than the last several years of persistent bull markets would suggest. And since the great bulk of total compensation for senior executives is share-related, the problem of excessive compensation levels may be partly, even largely, self-correcting one of these years.[2]

My final comment is to note that, while compensation questions are currently on the front burner, they have by no means come to a boil. In democracies, especially prosperous and relatively contented ones, change comes slowly and cautiously. As I said earlier in this chapter, talk about the French Revolution is not merely incendiary, it is absurd. But in a one-person, one-vote democracy, a sense of unfairness can persist and grow and lead eventually to redress. To reiterate, the mills of the gods grind slowly but....

STOCK OPTIONS FOR EXECUTIVES

The use of stock options as a central and integral component of Canadian executive compensation for public companies is already well established and continues to grow. Starting from the elementary assumption that bonuses help to motivate short-term performance, and some sort of stock grant or stock option helps to motivate longer-term performance, contemporary Canadian practice suggests that stock gains constitute about 25% of total compensation,

---

[2] This paragraph was written in late 1999. It's too easy a prediction to win any plaudits for prescience.

pre-tax. Obviously the percentage varies widely by industry and company but 25% isn't a bad midpoint over a full economic cycle. In the U.S. over that same cycle, the percentage was considerably higher, especially through most of the great bull market which ended in mid-2000. In the market conditions of late 2001, it's clear that many option and bonus payouts will be dramatically lower, both absolutely and as a percent of total executive compensation.

Growth in the use of options has outpaced that of outright grants. A company can provide far more options than shares per dollar of cost. The cost of the former is the gain alone and then only in terms of dilution, not net income. The cost of the latter is the full value of the shares and a direct hit to the bottom line.

Also, stock grants (or cash used to purchase shares) are not tax-effective in relation to options. Leveraged stock purchase programs can be tax-effective but have largely fallen out of favour because of several unfortunate experiences over the past several years. They are usually affected severely by economic cycles. By leveraged stock purchase plans, I mean those in which the employer offers low-interest or no-interest loans to key employees to purchase company shares. Any dividends are usually used to offset interest payments, real or assumed.

Since the liability is fixed, any major downward movement in the share price leaves the holder underwater and in debt, often deeply. The company's original intention— to motivate important contributors to corporate success— is subverted. In fact, employees can be demoralized with obvious negative impact on their performance.

Leveraged stock purchase plans make more sense in stable industries which aren't much exposed to economic cycles. Sadly, such industries are increasingly rare in an increasingly volatile universe.

Option plans are perceived in the market to be less affected since the downside is not an out-of-pocket cost but the opportunity cost of alternative cash income foregone. Moreover, the argument that option plans are unfair to shareholders (who suffer from cycles) is parried by the following. So long as the cost of options granted is an integral part of total compensation and so long as total compensation is fair and reasonable, based on objective comparative data, a failed option is a cost to the executive just as a share decline is a cost to the outside shareholder.

A subset of option plans worth mentioning is performance options. They are not yet common in Canada; a recent William Mercer analysis revealed that only 6 of the TSE 100 companies have performance features in their option plans. In the U.S., their use is somewhat more advanced, particularly over the past five years, though certainly not yet mainstream.

There are several variants. In one, the exercise price is set above market at the time of the grant. In another, some parallel goals must be met before the options vest. Typically, these goals are either external (e.g., the share price must exceed by some percentage the average share price of a representative peer group of companies) or internal (common goals include some level of ROE, operating income, net earnings, or cash flow).

In a third variation, options are granted with long vesting periods. If performance, measured by, say, EPS or ROI, exceeds certain targets, vesting is accelerated. This third variety appears not yet to have found its way into Canada.

With the TSE having relaxed its rules on the percentage of issued shares that can be applied to options, companies are reacting. Formerly, there was a straightforward limitation of 10%. Now, management and its board can go to the shareholders for approval of a number greater than 10%. Many companies have taken advantage of this with incentive shares as a percent of issued shares varying between 15% and in excess of 30%.

The justification for higher percentages varies but is usually either the need to compete for managers, particularly in high-tech industries (in Silicon Valley, options as a high percentage of total compensation have been a way of life), or the need to provide a higher ratio of variable to fixed compensation in smaller, high-risk, high-potential growth enterprises.

It's clear that institutional shareholders in Canada are sceptical about any trend towards exceeding 10%. My own view is that circumstances vary dramatically from company to company and there may well be cases where the 10% limit should be breached. It's management's job to make as persuasive a case as possible. Ultimately, the shareholders decide and, in this area, that is entirely appropriate.

Finally, a short, revealing anecdote illuminates the vast sea-change in the economic environment which began with the great Tech Wreck of mid-2000 and later and which had an as yet unquantified but directionally clear negative impact on senior executive compensation in 2001 and perhaps beyond.

Sometime in February of 2000, a *Newsweek* reporter interviewed Robert Rubin, then Secretary of the Treasury in the Clinton administration. Rubin, who has been described as the best U.S. Secretary of the Treasury since Alexander Hamilton, was asked this question: "Mr. Rubin, there are people who believe that new technology and globalization have repealed the business cycle... what's your view?"

To which Mr. Rubin's uncannily prophetic reply was: "There are people who believe that and it may turn out that they are right. But there is another possibility, which is that all of human history may turn out to be true instead. You just have to decide which you think is more likely."

That interview took place before the first cracks appeared in the foundations of the dot-com wonderland and a year before the broader stock market began to falter and weaken.

At least for a year or two, executive compensation will be severely affected in many industries and companies by the firestorm of bad news which followed soon after Mr. Rubin's astute observations.

SOME CURRENT ISSUES WITH STOCK OPTIONS

The Economist of August 7, 1999, told a little story which characterizes today's executive compensation world:

"Once upon an Arabian night, sultans were paid their weight in gold. Today, such an approach to pay would leave the typical boss of a large American company sorely disappointed. Bosses now prefer to be paid in share options, which are far more valuable than mere metal. Tipping the scales—let's be kind and ignore those boardroom lunches —at 200 pounds, and with gold now at about $258 a troy ounce, the average CEO of one of American's top 200 firms would take home over $750,000 in gold. In fact, in 1998 he made a pre-tax profit of $8.3 million by exercising executive share options. At the end of last year, he also had total unrealized gains of nearly $50 million."

The price of gold has changed a bit from then to now and perhaps CEO avoirdupois is a tad overstated but the essence of the story is disturbingly valid. All dollar figures are in U.S. currency; add about 60% for Canadian audiences at date of writing.

This story provides a natural lead-in to the focus of this section, namely, a discussion of some of the more contentious issues surrounding option plans. When people use the word "excessive" in discussing executive compensation, it is clearly the option component which is both the most lucrative and the most controversial and open to criticism.

Four aspects merit attention of which the first is the ubiquitous Black-Scholes model for valuing options. A recent ground-breaking study by two senior compensation consultants with Towers and Perrin reached some very interesting and, if validated, important conclusions.

As is widely known, the Black-Scholes formula, developed by Nobel Prize winner Fischer Black and his colleague, Myron Scholes, was developed to value short-term options, i.e., publicly-traded stock options with a life of one to six months. Here Black-Scholes has proved its worth thousands of times over. Unfortunately, it has been pressed into much wider service for setting a value on long-term option grants to corporate executives. The

McMillan-Brown research concludes that the Black-Scholes model systematically undervalues long-term options, leading boards to grant more options than needed or justified.

Most executive stock option grants have a ten-year life; few have a life shorter than five years. The most important variable in valuing such long-term options is anticipated long-term stock price appreciation. And Black-Scholes is not at all helpful in predicting this. In fact, it doesn't even try. The McMillan-Brown study concluded:

"If a company grants options based on a 30% Black-Scholes ratio, and achieves its targeted long term stock price appreciation of 10% per annum, it would have granted more than three times as many options as were required to deliver the intended level of pay."

If further analysis confirms this conclusion, a major re-evaluation of the quantum of option grants is clearly needed.

The second issue worth discussing is option repricing. To repeat what I said in an earlier chapter, my view is simplicity itself: never, never, never. Perhaps there is a circumstance when repricing is fully acceptable but I confess that I can't think of one, though I've tried.

Nevertheless, the practice is rather popular. When share prices fell quite sharply in the late summer of 1998, many firms (again to quote *The Economist*) "repriced their options just in time to enjoy massive gains when the market rebounded" later that autumn and winter.

To give a more specific example, 17 U.S. firms in the financial services industry lowered their strike prices in the autumn of 1998 by one-third. Not long after, their share prices had, on average, tripled.

Some firms attempt to justify repricing by lowering the number of options re-granted so that the net present value of the new grant is the same as the net present value of the original grant. While I concede that this is more acceptable than merely offering the same number of options as before but at a new and lower market price, I'm still negative on principle. Allow me to repeat my generalized mantra: Repricing of any kind gives the executive a second chance; unfortunately, shareholders who buy and sell at market do not have such an opportunity.

The third issue worthy of comment is the current accounting treatment of options. Bizarre though current practice is, the cost of options in both the U.S. and Canada is still not reflected in income statements in any way. This assumes that shares made available to option holders upon exercise come from treasury, as is normally the case.

The only exception to this accounting anomaly is itself perverse. In the U.S., performance options, where there's no payoff unless performance exceeds one or more pre-agreed norms (internal, external, or a mix), are costed and charged against income. Partly for this reason and partly because corporate managements are not usually enamoured of the more demanding hurdles which must be met for there to be a payoff, performance options are greatly underutilized.

It's unfortunate and dysfunctional that mediocrity is too frequently rewarded, while superior performance is penalized.

I cannot resist adding that, when accounting rules inhibit the use of an incentive tool which most executives would prefer to avoid, there's at least a hint that the accounting profession serves industry in more ways than one.

The Sage of Omaha, as clear-headed an investor as exists, put it in his usual succinct way when he wrote in Berkshire Hathaway's annual report:

"Accounting principles offer management a choice: pay employees in one form and count the cost, or pay them in another form and ignore the cost. Small wonder then that the use of options has mushroomed. If options aren't a form of compensation, what are they? If compensation isn't an expense, what is it? And, if expenses shouldn't go into the calculation of earnings, where in the world should they go?"

Finally, in case there's any doubt about the magnitude of the impact on income statements caused by the current accounting treatment of options, let me cite an example. It is well-known that high-tech firms use options more frequently and generously than most industries, at least partly because, in their start-up phases, cash is the scarce resource. It has been reported by a British research firm that Microsoft, with one of the largest market caps in the world and which earned $4.5 billion in 1998, would have lost $18 billion if the cost of options awarded that year plus that year's increase in the value of options already out-standing had been fully charged against income. This may be an extreme case but it's disturbing nevertheless.

The same order of magnitude effect would have been found in the next two years. Options are a way of life at firms like Microsoft and it explains why expensing options when granted would have a profound effect on the recorded earnings of many companies.

My summary conclusion on this issue is that present accounting practice in North America is not merely highly misleading; it lies somewhere along the border between outlandish and bizarre. The accounting profession, goaded to some extent by regulators, is re-evaluating current practice; some changes are highly likely, though I doubt that they will confront the central issue head-on but rather more peripherally and obliquely.

Finally, I'd like to go into a bit more depth on the subject of performance options. While there are an almost infinite number of variations in the details, there are two quite different types of performance options. Let me define each.

Category I is where a performance hurdle, either absolute or relative, must be met before options can be exercised. The hurdle can be internal (like exceeding an ROE, ROI, EPS goal) or it can be external (like the share price reaching a pre-agreed level or rising faster than either some broad market index or a more industry-specific index). The important point is that, if the performance hurdle is met, all option gains above strike price at market are realized. That is, the hurdle is a go/no go barrier which determines whether any option gains are paid or not but does not affect the amount of those gains.

Category II is where option gains start at the level of the performance hurdle which, again, can be either internal or external, absolute or relative, or some mix thereof. For example, assume the performance hurdle is that the company must do better than the average share price performance of a representative group of peer companies. The option gains are zero at the point where the company and its peer group have equivalent share price performance. Only performance better than the hurdle—in this example, the average of peer group performance—is rewarded.

Obviously performance options in Category I are more remunerative than those in Category II, other things (like the number of options granted) being equal.

Not surprisingly, U.S. firms have almost overwhelmingly shied away from performance options of any stripe, let alone those in Category II. The Economist's line, "American firms have mostly run a mile from share options designed to reward market-beating or above-average performance," is an accurate assessment. Executives are loath to see any deterioration in their performance/reward matrix. That this reluctance is compounded by accounting rules which militate against performance options is theatre of the absurd.

A cool reception to performance options is hardly surprising. This is demonstrated dramatically by a study conducted by Graef Crystal, that implacable critic of executive compensation excess. He calculated the impact of an option plan in which executives cannot exercise their options unless share prices rise more than the S&P 500 index. Note that, if prices do meet the hurdle, option gains are from strike price upwards. In other words, it's a Category I plan. Crystal showed that, for all S&P 500 companies between 1995 and 1998, a conventional option plan would have rewarded 86% of CEOs with an average gain of $8 million each. With the performance option plan, 68% of these same CEOs would have received exactly nothing.

For performance options to move into the mainstream, some combination of institutional investors (too many of whom, but not all, are still sleeping giants), external auditors (to provide a level playing field for options, regardless of type), tough compensation committees (sometimes an oxymoron but, fortunately, not always), and regulators (who have less clout in some areas than is generally recognized) needs to coalesce and take action.

The reformation of how executives are paid cries for the elimination of windfall gains—sometimes extraordinary in amount—made by all too many executives for doing nothing more than matching the average performance of stock prices in an ebullient bull market of unprecedented longevity, since ended, though beginning in early 2002 to pave the ground again, if somewhat tentatively.

Many good friends, especially senior line executives, accuse me from time to time of taking too hard a line on options. Maybe. But the game's name still is or certainly ought to be producing as much shareholder value as is compatible with operating an enterprise ethically and honestly. I submit that some recent and current option practices go well beyond fairness and into the transfer of wealth from shareholders to managements in an unwarranted and unprecedented way.

EXECUTIVE PENSIONS

This section is based on a speech given to a seminar sponsored by The Canadian Institute on the topic: "Executive Pensions At Risk"

Let me recount to you a story I heard the other day. It actually has a connection, albeit a tenuous one, to executive pensions. It's about a skeleton found recently in an attic cupboard in a large old house being demolished in rural England. Around the skeleton's bony neck was a chain with a medal on it inscribed "Hide and seek champion: 1910."

So what's the connection to Supplemental Executive Retirement Plans (SERPs)? Put simply, it's this:

• The world is unpredictable and often hostile.

• Don't count on government to solve your problems.

• Look after yourself; no one else will.

In playing a key role in the corporate decision-making process, all directors are exposed to various claims of various constituencies. First and foremost, of course, they represent the interests of the shareholders. But they must also be concerned with managerial and employee interests and concerns as well as those of other stakeholders, including customers, suppliers, the community, and the public interest more broadly. As a minimum, the interests of these other stakeholders constitutes a set of constraints on the interests of the shareholder as the central and dominant stakeholder. Some academicians and other theorists would go further than this. I don't, but I do agree that all interests have to be considered to some degree in any board decision.

Let me begin with a basic assumption: in an ideal world, an individual who works 35 years for a company with a 2% defined benefit plan should retire with a pension of 70% of final pre-retirement income, recognizing that such final income can be defined in various ways.

Obviously, the fairness and affordability of this 70% rule of thumb depend on a host of factors, such as age of retirement; average length of time between retirement and death; whether the plan is indexed partly or fully, contractually or voluntarily; the cost of living in the community of retirement in relation to the community of active employment; and at least a dozen other factors which any alert actuary can recite without difficulty.

However, let's agree on 70% as a reasonable objective and then let's look at what happens to five individuals with five different final earnings levels.

Before drawing any conclusions from this table, permit me a couple of qualifying comments. First, there are plenty of defined benefit plans less generous than the 2% plan used in the calculations and very few more generous, at least not in the private sector. Some government plans for members of parliament or legislative assemblies are essentially 4% plans with full indexing. Plans for senior civil servants are less generous but still far superior to the typical private-sector plan. The twin public-sector abominations of double-dipping and pensions starting years before normal retirement age have been widely condemned in recent years. Indeed a few steps here and there have been taken to eliminate or at least moderate these repellent practices.

IMPACT OF SERPS ON PENSIONS BY SIZE

Final Earnings for Pension Purposes	$30,000	*$86,111	$150,000	$500,000	1,000,000
Pension with a Registered Retirement Plan (A 2% Plan and Assuming 35 Years' Service)	21,000	60,277	60,277	60,277	60,277
Pension as a % of Final Earnings	70	70	40	12	6
Pension Which Includes a SERP to Bring Pension to 70% of Final Earnings	21,000	60,277	105,000	350,000	700,000
Annual Contribution of SERP to Pension	0	0	44,723	289,723	639,723

Maximum final earnings to provide maximum pension under an RRP of $60,277 ($1,722.22 x 35 years of service)

A few private-sector plans, but only a few, provide full, contractual indexing. Far more common are plans with periodic indexing at management and board discretion. Usually these are indexed at 50% to 60% of CPI and adjusted every 3 or 4 years.

Another point to note is that the $60,277 of maximum pension under an RPP is fixed until the year 2005 after which it will be indexed in line with the average industrial wage. In that year, it will be the equivalent of $49,000 in current dollar terms if inflation averages 2% per year and of $44,800 if inflation averages 3%. So the problem of pensions starting at 70% of final earnings and then gradually falling below it over time is further exacerbated.

Allow me now to draw a conclusion or two from the data presented. The perspective will still be that of a company director.

First, from the viewpoint of equity and ignoring temporarily the important matter of affordability, there is something unfair about providing post-retirement income equal to 70% of pre-retirement income for people earning up to $86,111, as well as for others at the top of the company hierarchy while allowing those many persons in between to retire on pensions which are significantly below the 70% rule of thumb for employees with 35 years' service.

For companies without SERPs or with SERPs restricted to a small number of executives at or near the top of an organization, the drop in income can be dramatic. For someone whose final pensionable earnings are $150,000, the drop is 60%; at $500,000 it's 88%; at $1,000,000, it's 94%.

While it doesn't appear that any systematic study has yet been conducted, there is some evidence to suggest that perhaps 60% or as high as two-thirds of the TSE 300 companies have SERPs of one kind or another. Obviously this means that at least one-third of this group have no SERPs at all.

Furthermore, for non-TSE 300 companies, which tend to be smaller, newer, more entrepreneurial, and operating in high-tech or resource-based industries, the percentage without SERPS is considerably higher, perhaps in the 75% range.

Of course, some companies, whether part of the TSE 300 list or not, which don't provide SERPs do offer alternative incentives, such as generous bonuses or stock option plans. These provide their recipients with the opportunity to supplement their post-retirement income. Unfortunately, it's all too easy to spend discretionary income when it's earned rather than saving it for the future, especially before age 50 when current demands on income are high and retirement is far enough into the future to be largely out of mind.

It is also fairly obvious that, at $1,000,000 of pensionable earnings, the individual can look after himself without much additional company assistance in the form of a SERP.

But that's not where the more serious problem lies. Of these companies which do provide SERPs, 68% have cut-offs. That is, the highest-paid six to ten executives in a typical company have SERPs but no-one else does. It is true that the larger the company, the lower the percentage which impose cut-offs. For example, 61% of companies with 500 or more employees have cut-offs. That is still a lot of companies.

Managements and boards face a difficult, no-win situation. They want to act fairly and they want to attract and hold the best middle and senior managers. A company without a SERP may feel it is necessary to introduce one. And a company with a highly exclusive SERP may be forced to reduce or even eliminate the restrictions.

However, in taking these steps, such companies obviously face increased costs. Depending on the specifics, these costs can be considerable. In an increasingly competitive global environment, this cannot be ignored.

If the SERP liabilities are funded in the sense that the company earmarks dollars for this specific purpose, the expense, which is not tax-effective, affects profits. If an RCA (Retirement Compensation Arrangement) is used, the cost is deductible but the RCA itself pays a 50% tax. Letters of credit are expensive and, like D & O insurance, work best when not needed.

From an employer perspective, the least expensive approach, especially for companies with tax loss carryforwards (but even for companies without any), is pay as you go. Particularly with a fairly young workforce, the payment is deferred until the SERP participant retires and then, of course, it's tax deductible.

However, from the perspective of the employee, an unsecured, unfunded SERP has a questionable value. It does not carry a lot of weight with, say, a 45-year-old executive who is considering a job change. In calculating his net worth, he discounts heavily the value of this kind of SERP. This shouldn't be surprising. A company can go belly-up and an unsecured SERP becomes worthless except in the unlikely event that enough can be salvaged from the wreckage. Some companies in some industries are, of course, less vulnerable than others.

Or a company can be taken over by an institution determined to reduce costs. That institution is, of course, normally responsible for the past-service liabilities associated with a SERP but can, if it wishes, decide to reduce or even eliminate those all-important future-service liabilities. This is the so-called "change of heart," a memorable phrase used by a well-known Toronto-based pension and insurance specialist.

So, despite both the complexity and the cost of various approaches to securing SERPs, there is a small but growing percentage of companies which are moving in this direction.

A William Mercer survey conducted a few years ago found that 82% of SERPs were unfunded, 14% used RCAs, and 4% used letters of credit or insurance-based schemes. But since there's little point in providing an expensive benefit which is unappreciated, it's fairly likely that secured SERPs will grow faster over the next decade than the pay-as-you-go variety. Of course this raises the cost of the SERP still further but there is a fair amount of evidence to support the view that the incremental value to the employee is considerably greater than the incremental cost to the company.

Will government come to the financial aid of pension plans in some way? Don't even think about it. The chances of government improving the tax-deductibility of pensions in general, SERPs in particular, are next to zero.

In fact, the odds are greater that the government will tighten the rules further, in line with recent changes already announced. For example, the last time the annual pension limit per year of service was changed was in 1976, when it was increased from $1,143 to $1,715 and, more recently, to $1,722, a miniscule gain of less than 1/2%. The next change will take place in 2005 unless delayed even further. As noted earlier, it will be indexed at the rate of change of the average industrial wage.

To count on further relief from government to make SERPs more tax-effective is to tilt at windmills. The present federal government's priorities are to continue to reduce taxes to more internationally competitive levels, to preserve our national health system, to enhance the quality of education, and to use any remaining surplus to reduce the national debt.

So with SERPs as with so many issues in the modern industrial or post-industrial world, we have the usual cast of players. Employees have one set of priorities and shareholders have another. They intersect at various points but are quite different at others. And then there's the board and senior management seeking to mediate among conflicting claims on the corporate purse.

Employees want a level of pension income that avoids punishing them with too sharp a drop from pre-retirement earnings. And they want that income secured against either business failure or takeover and that change of heart.

As if it weren't obvious, the shareholder wants some combination of increasing capital appreciation and dividends. That same shareholder is acutely aware that, in an intensely competitive global economy, this means strict control of expenses as an absolutely necessary though insufficient component of satisfactory performance.

To sum up, the extension of SERPs to embrace all employees earning more than $86,111 of final earnings is expensive and, if payments are to be made secure and tamper-proof, the cost is higher still. As I said, don't count on governments for relief. They have their own priorities and these do not include providing extra tax deductions to corporations to support managers earning more than $86,000. Clawing back previous tax concessions is more likely.

And there in the middle are the board and the CEO, buffeted by all the opposing pulls. If I were to attempt a pension forecast for the next ten years, while recognizing that we live in an increasingly unpredictable and even discontinuous world, it would come in four parts.

First, SERPs will increase as a percent of all pension plans but with no further help from government.

Second, within any given pension plan, a higher percent of employees will be part of a SERP. In time, Registered Pension Plans (RPPs) and SERPs will, in effect, merge into a seamless continuum. The only meaningful distinction will be the tax effectiveness of one and not the other.

Third, wherever possible, companies will be looking for every way to maximize the pensions available from tax-effective and secure RPPs in order to shift some of the burden of costs away from the tax-ineffective SERP.

Finally, the funding of SERPs will continue to grow apace. That is, a benefit that isn't valued by the potential recipient is likely to be replaced by one that is. Less expensive ways to fund will be sought and found.

Some Personal Experiences as a Director (III)

In this ongoing recital of personal experiences as a director over more than three decades, I'd like to describe two situations which involved corporate insolvency. One had a happy, even triumphant, ending; the other didn't. I'll begin with the one that didn't. (I always prefer to close on an upbeat note).

Interlink Freight Systems, mentioned earlier, was the new name adopted after Canadian Pacific sold one of its largest and oldest trucking operations—CP Express and Transport—to its 3000 employees in 1994.

Ten percent of the shares were sold to management, 20% to the non-unionized office employees, and 70% to the many unionized employees. The shares of this last group were held in trust by the Transportation and Communications Union (TCU), which voted them on behalf of their owners.

The board consisted of three senior members of management, three union representatives, and five independent directors (of which I was one). I was also board chairman. Of the three union representatives, one was an employee, one was a retired president of the national union, and one was a high-profile union leader in an unrelated field.

The company functioned for just over two years but eventually went into that "long winter out of which there's no spring." Interlink is now nothing but a memory and, at least in some circles, not an especially fond one.

There are two clear lessons here. Any constituency board is extremely difficult to manage well. Certainly I never fully succeeded as chairman in getting all directors to pray from the same breviary. Second, a union finds it difficult, if not impossible, to separate its role as a representative of the controlling shareholders and owners from its role as a representative of organized labour. It is constantly torn between its traditional role of representing workers *qua* workers and its rather more unfamiliar role of representing workers *qua* shareholders and capitalists.

Whether the company could somehow have surmounted this formidable hurdle is hard to say. In spinning off its unwanted trucking subsidiary, Canadian Pacific had not been generous with its contribution to the capitalization of Interlink as a free-standing enterprise.

The waters were muddied further by the fact that there were also difficult business issues. Adoption of NAFTA and consequent closer economic integration of the U.S. and

Canada shifted the locus of freight movement from east-west within Canada to north-south and across the U.S. border. This exposed Interlink to intensified competition from larger, more sophisticated companies, not all of which were unionized.

Those who dislike constituency boards will argue that Interlink was felled by insufficient single-minded commitment to profit generation. Their argument is supported by the fact that labour costs were by far the largest expense component. In the highly competitive transport world, productivity is a crucial variable. And while some productivity gains were achieved, they were not enough and they could have been greater.

Those who believe that the real culprit was a rapidly changing and deteriorating business environment will argue that the Interlink story makes no useful comment on the efficacy of constituency boards. My own view is that both factors contributed to Interlink's demise in roughly equal proportions.

And now to my other descent into the murky world of insolvency. Silcorp limited, a successor company to the venerable Silverwood Dairies, was controlled by a family, facilitated by a dual share class structure. For various reasons, including an unsuccessful foray into the convenience store market in Tidewater Virginia, the company slid slowly towards insolvency and sought protection under CCAA during the sharp recession of the early nineties.

After nearly a year of excruciatingly difficult decisions and heavy fees to lawyers, investment bankers, and bankruptcy experts, the company emerged from CCAA but in thrall at the outset to creditors: principally bond holders, commercial bankers, and suppliers.

In 1993, the stock was relisted on the TSE at an open-
ing price of $2 per share. The Findlay family had by then
lost control. Derek Ridout, appointed as CEO in April 1992,
just prior to CCAA, continued in that role along with a
new chairman, Bob Martin, who had led the restructuring
committee. The board combined a few of the old-guard
directors, including me, and several new members, most of
them representing institutional shareholders and creditors
or bringing relevant new skills to the boardroom table.

Over the next five years, the company went from
strength to strength, virtually re-inventing itself inside and
out. It defeated a hostile takeover bid by Couche-Tard, a
Quebec-based convenience store company. It acquired a
substantial competitor, the Becker Milk Company, along
with several hundred new stores. In 1999, it entered into
what had morphed into friendly talks with the same
Couche-Tard, a company which combined an insatiable
desire to enter the Ontario and western Canada markets
with the financial resources to pay full price for the very
profitable business Silcorp had become.

As a result of strong leadership, the company had grown
and prospered to the point where, in May of 1999, Couche-
Tard paid $46 per share (after adjusting for a stock split) to
Silcorp shareholders. A twenty-three fold increase in share
price in five years may look modest in relation to some of
the more spectacular (pre-flame out!) dot-com stories. But
old-fashioned investors like Peter Lynch would call it a 23-
bagger, nearly six times better than a mere home run.

Here the lesson is obvious. Strong management, working closely with a strong board led by an excellent chairman, found the will, the perseverance, and the street
smarts to reject a premature and inadequate hostile bid.

But it also had the wisdom and the sense of timing to accept a later and eminently satisfactory friendly bid. There's a time to hold them and a time to fold them. A happy ending all around.

I cannot resist adding, as a postcript comment, that there are few things more frustrating than a director's role during CCAA. Much of the process is dominated and even controlled by various classes of experts representing various constituencies and plying their respective trades at what some would call extortionate rates. It is, I suppose, the inevitable ransom paid by a management and board for allowing a corporation to slip into CCAA in the first place.

PART 4

The Rubber Meets the Road:

Challenges Facing Corporations

CHAPTER 11

Corporate Responsibility

This chapter is based on a speech given fairly recently at the downtown campus of the Schulich School of Business of York University in Toronto. It addresses a pivotal, if not the central, question facing directors and management of profit-seeking enterprises: To whom do they owe their duty? In whose interests are they working?

In traditional jurisprudence, the answer at the first level of enquiry is clear. It's the corporation. This leads to a much harder question: "Who is the corporation?"

To take one end of the spectrum of views, the Delaware courts have affirmed time and time again that, for corporations registered in that state, directors and officers have a fiduciary duty to maximize shareholder wealth. That is, the Delaware courts have explicitly equated the interests of the corporation with those of its shareholders. To foreshadow a point I want to make later, note that the courts are silent on the time-line for maximizing shareholder returns.

Outside of Delaware, the historical view of the courts is less directive. It too requires the corporation to maximize profits, again without imposing a time-frame, but it does not define the corporation as the agent of the shareholders in the explicit way that Delaware does.

There is an instructive legal case, Dodge v. Ford Motor Company,[1] which dates back to 1919. Henry Ford, as majority shareholder, had not wanted to pay dividends because he wished to direct all the cash he could lay his hands on to a program of capacity expansion. In arguing for this in a suit launched by some minority shareholders, Mr. Ford noted that expansion would lead to lower costs, lower prices, higher sales due to elasticity of demand, and eventually higher profits. So far, so good.

Unfortunately, he chose to emphasize that his motives for the expansion were at least partly altruistic, based on the premise that lower prices would put automobile ownership within the reach of people further down the income scale.

The Supreme Court of Michigan criticized Mr. Ford's social policy rationale for expansion, saying, "If Mr. Ford wants to pursue such goals, he should do it with his own money, not the corporation's."

---

[1] I am indebted to an article by Mr. James Hanks in the September/October, 1996 issue of *The Journal of Corporate Governance* (U.S.) for his views on this case as well as his views on Delaware legislation more generally.

In short, it was not the action to forego a dividend nor the related decision to expand which aroused the court's disapproval but any inference that some motive other than or even in addition to profit maximization influenced the decision-making process. Viewing the customer as a stakeholder was beyond the pale, or so it now appears eighty-three years after the fact.

At the other end of the spectrum of views on the question of who the corporation is in aid of is the stakeholder theory. It has waxed and waned over the past sixty years or so and has many proponents today. Some of them are passionate and tireless advocates of the position that the shareholder is only one of several claimants on the corporation's accumulated wealth. The litany of other claimants includes employees, suppliers, customers, the local community, the environment, and the national interest.

What being a claimant means in the operational sense is frequently obscure and even contradictory. Nevertheless, the stakeholder model of corporate governance is one with emotional appeal and many adherents. Over 25 U.S. states passed laws in the second half of the eighties, permitting boards of directors to *consider* the interests of persons other than the corporations and its shareholders.

These stakeholder statutes were supported by many boards and managements, not for altruistic reasons but, more disingenuously, because they could be useful as a defense against takeovers. That is, they gave boards and management broader grounds on which to reject a hostile takeover bid. Even if a bid was attractive in price terms to shareholders, board and management could justify rejection using arguments like the best interests of employees, the continuity of the enterprise, and the economic vitality of communities hosting plant sites. The entrenchment of management and the board was, of course, rarely broached as a rationale.

A more modest and middle-of-the-road view, one to which I subscribe, is that the interests of constituencies or stakeholders other than shareholders may be taken into account provided that, as the Delaware high court phrased it rather delicately in a well-known case, there is "some reasonable relationship to general shareholder interests."

But let us be clear. Catering to these other interests is not a co-objective. Such interests ought not to rank *pari passu* with shareholder interests. At times they constitute legitimate constraints on shareholder interests although even that depends on the circumstances.

To repeat, the enhancement of stakeholder interests, from the perspective of the board and management, may be defensible and useful as an argument to protect the best interests of the corporation, even though such interests may appear at times (especially in the short run) to be incongruent with the best interests of its shareholders.

The use of the phrase "especially in the short run" brings us to a crucial issue. Over what time-frame are we considering and measuring the best interests of the corporation, of its shareholders, and of its other stakeholders?

Even in Delaware, the jurisdiction most strongly in favour of shareholder rights, the State Supreme Court recognized two important principles in the classic Time Warner case:

(a) The fiduciary duty to manage a corporate enterprise includes the selection of a time-frame for meeting corporate goals.

(b) Directors must chart a course for a corporation which is in its best interests without regard to a fixed investment horizon.

These two principles support what I consider to be a contemporary mainstream view. That is, it may be appropriate at times for a board and management to deviate from short-run shareholder interests in favour of longer-run corporate interests if the intent is full compatibility with longer-run shareholder interests.

Despite continuing criticism, the decision to take a long-term view on some issues and when competitive forces permit is widespread. And it is supported by a broad phalanx[2] of informed observers who deplore decision-making predicated solely on what the stock price is going to do when the next statement of quarterly earnings is released.

Shareholders vary enormously in their goals and needs and in the time-frame over which they wish to realize these. We have the arbs with a time-span of anywhere from a few hours to a few days. We have institutional investors who should take a longer view but sometimes don't. At one extreme is the Oracle of Omaha, who seeks out stocks like Coca-Cola and holds them for decades. Then there are the pension funds who, despite long-tailed liabilities, expect the investment managers they hire to perform no worse than second quartile—and preferably first—in both strong markets and weak. This puts enormous pressure on these managers to worry excessively about the short run. And who can blame them?

[2] The phalanx seemed to shrink somewhat in the waning of the twentieth century when irrational exuberance led to widespread acceptance of the dictum that long-term is the day after tomorrow.

Then there are the widows and orphans and retired folk generally, who want income and are risk-averse. And the upwardly mobile executive for whom the name of the game is capital gain. And the young family which is somewhere in the middle. I could go on naming categories but won't.

Because shareholders have widely varying investment objectives, boards and managements sometimes have the freedom to take a longer view of how best to maximize shareholder wealth. A classic example is how best to respond to a hostile takeover. But to go beyond long-run corporate interests (remembering that even here it's possible to deviate from the interests of some shareholders some of the time) is to get into murky waters indeed.

Which brings me back to the so-called "stakeholder model," in which parties other than the shareholder and other than by contract have some ill-defined claim on a corporation's net worth, its residual accumulated wealth.

In 1996, the Clinton administration sponsored a conference on corporate responsibility. Many Fortune 500 CEOs attended; the event attracted a great deal of media attention. Even after making adjustments for the fact that some business leaders may have gotten a little carried away by the atmosphere of an election year and so may have told the sponsors some of what they wanted to hear, the responses were surprising.

Mr. Gerald Greenwald, the CEO of United Airlines, argued persuasively that there are rarely, if ever, valid reasons for corporate downsizing. It's worth noting here that United has significant employee ownership. However, he was apparently supported by several other CEOs who agreed that downsizing was doing a great deal of harm both to the economy and to corporate reputations.

Such sentiments might appear to fly in the face of the conventional wisdom that it's often "downsize or perish" but they still fall under the rubric of enhancing long-term corporate interests. They place a value on loyalty and morale and public attitudes and on the simple reality that every employee is also a consumer, at least at the level of the economy as a whole.

With downsizing or any other contentious issue, some companies will balance the trade-offs one way and choose a policy. Others will use a different calculus and embrace a different policy. But each decision-maker is motivated always by a vision of what is in the best long-term interests of the corporation, which is almost invariably also in the best long-term interests of its shareholders (or at least some and often most of them).

To go further than this, as some "stakeholder model" advocates at the most radical end of the spectrum argue, is to borrow big trouble. Should a corporation pay more than prevailing wages unless justified by more-than-prevailing performance? Should a corporation pay its suppliers more than the lowest price it can negotiate for comparable quality? Should it sell its products for less than the market is willing to pay? Should it ignore legal tax avoidance measures, and pay more taxes than required? Should it shun government subsidies? Should it provide financial support to civic projects unless justified by realistic forecasts of marketing value or goodwill created?

While the answer to these questions is usually "no," it depends, once again, on a best estimate in each unique case of what's best for a given corporation on a time-line that a board and a management have chosen.

What it does not depend on is some quixotic impulse to redistribute a company's earnings or net worth to claimants with no more legitimacy than a shopper looking at expensive watches in a window at Cartier's.

To go further, and perhaps I'm belabouring the obvious, is to place a corporation and all who depend on it in jeopardy. For a corporate executive, this is the deadliest of deadly sins alleviated only by the reality that any management pursuing such a course is unlikely to survive long enough to do irreparable harm.

Enlightened self-interest, the mainstay of a free market economy, must be allowed to function. The alternative would thrust directors and management into a fuzzy, amorphous, shapeless world. I would have added "unexplored" but three-quarters of a century of collectivism in Russia was exploration enough.

MORE ON SHAREHOLDER VS STAKEHOLDER CAPITALISM

One aspect of the broader topic of corporate responsibility in today's world is the choice between two competing ideologies: shareholder capitalism and stakeholder capitalism.

With shareholder capitalism, the primary objective of board and management is straightforward; it's to serve the best interests of shareholders. This is not to say that other stakeholders do not represent legitimate constraints on shareholder best interests. Clearly they do. To take a simple example, many concerns about the environment must be heeded. This starts with obeying the law but often extends beyond it. The law is rarely the best arbiter of appropriate corporate behaviour; it is often too little and invariably too late.

But, regardless of the issue and despite the legitimacy of any of a wide range of claims on the corporate purse, the objective function—the *only* objective function—is serving the shareholder.

You will notice that, in discussing shareholder capitalism, I am avoiding the term "profit maximization." Not only does this carry heavy emotional baggage but it is, in any event, a bogeyman. By that I mean that almost no company practices it in its pure or extreme form. Chainsaw Al Dunlop at Scott Paper, then, later, at Sunbeam, came close for a time, but we saw what happened to him.

Shareholder capitalism does encompass and permit taking a longer-run view of the time-frame over which shareholder interests are to be served. Of course, the definition of "longer-run" is itself conjectural. As some pundit once observed, the future isn't what it used to be. And it's also unlikely to be what we think it will be. Forecasts over a longer period than, say, three years are too often monuments to our inability to comprehend the future in an era of unprecedented change, an era marked by both discontinuities and capriciousness.

So, while there's nothing wrong with the principle of giving up profits today in order to earn enhanced profits tomorrow, the calculus is murky. Or, as "Dubya" famously said in a debate with Al Gore, "The arithmetic is fuzzy."

I might add that some decisions which are justified as supporting long-run shareholder interest are, in fact, acts of altruism, at least in part. Charitable donations provide a good example.

Advocates of the purest variety of shareholder capitalism object strenuously to charitable donations, which are
perceived as venturing beyond even long-term shareholder
interests. The economist Milton Friedman, now in his
ninetieth year, has argued strenuously for years that shareholders who wish to support charitable causes—no matter
how deserving—should do so directly and personally
rather than have it done for them involuntarily through
corporate giving.

A middle-of-the-road position and one I certainly support is some cautious and carefully considered divergence
from short-term in favour of longer-term profits if, but
only if, some reasonable case can be made that shareholder
interests are truly served. Reasonable, like beauty, is, of
course, in the eye of the beholder. What seems reasonable to me may look outlandishly foolish to you. So sound
judgement is at least as important as the numbers and the
calculations.

Furthermore, attempting to take a longer-run view is
hindered by the financial community's stubborn and
mostly irrational overemphasis on the next quarter. As
the relationship between earnings and share prices moved
to ever more unsustainable levels in recent years, edgi-
ness became the norm and, not surprisingly, this led to a
focus on the less-risky immediate. (Whether the ongoing
market correction of the past year or so and still count-
ing will change this myopic focus remains to be seen. I'm
dubious.)

Turn now to stakeholder capitalism. In its pure and
undiluted version, just about every constituency with an
interest becomes a co-stakeholder. This includes all the
usual groups: customers; suppliers; employees; the public

interest in general, as represented by various levels of government as well as by a vast coterie of public-interest groups; the environment in particular; and, oh yes, the shareholder, who may be *primus inter pares* on some issues but definitely not on most.

In fact, I don't overstate the case when I say that advocates of the more radical brand of stakeholder capitalism seem, in practice, to rank shareholders at or near the bottom of the list of claimants on the corporate purse—or at least lower than *their* claims.

Now I don't want to sound like one of those infamous two-handed economists who took a lot of ribbing from Pierre Trudeau. So let me tell you where I stand on this vexed issue. Two decades ago, I believed that the concept of stakeholder capitalism, that is, the notion of co-stakeholders, had appeal and merit.

Now, older, though I hope not sunk into ideological rigidity and knee-jerk reactionism, I have come to believe that the pure co-stakeholder model is impracticable. By that I mean that it is impossible to practise in any widespread way in our highly competitive, free enterprise world. And the fact that almost no corporation does practise it suggests that the half-life of any corporation which attempts to is ominously short.

But there's more to it than that. In his thoughtful book, *Capitalism for Tomorrow*, Allen Sykes quotes Graham Serjeants' perceptive line: "For you will search in vain for companies whose shareholders languish yet whose other stakeholders prosper."

By extension, this means that, if the shareholder prospers, the odds are greater that so too will other stakeholders.

To all but the most partisan protagonists of the most radical version of stakeholder capitalism, this quote makes an important point. That is, and ironically, shareholder capitalism is more likely than stakeholder capitalism to satisfy *all* stakeholders. As a single example, job creation and job elimination take place, for the most part, in profitable and unprofitable enterprises, respectively.

CHAPTER 12

Institutional Investors

Should society be concerned about the growing muscle-flexing of institutional investors in regard to companies in which they hold shares? In Corporate Governance 101, management answers to the board and the board answers to the shareholders. This is a sound statement of principle but, as with so many things, practice isn't quite as simple as theory. In the world of realpolitick, employees, management, the board of directors, the shareholders including institutional investors, and several other groups less central to my argument each have some power and considerable self-interest.

For the business world to function effectively, there must be as much congruence of interest as possible among the various sets of players, using a wide range of influences including the law, compensation and other policies, effective management, the power of persuasion, the development of a coherent culture, and so on.

Let me examine briefly the interests of each of the principal players in the world of corporate governance and the allegiances which they form.

Consider first the employees of a company but excluding management. If they identify with anything these days, it's with the company itself, though downsizing over the past decade or so has weakened the bonds of loyalty. Many employees are increasingly sceptical about identifying their interests too closely with those of their employer or, as one disillusioned ex-employee put it a few years ago, "Never love a corporation, for it will never love you back."

Nevertheless, the employee's paycheque comes from the company and, though worried about job security and perhaps a little jaundiced about the increasing gap between senior executive compensation and his own, he aligns himself more with his company than, for example, with the more remote board of directors or the amorphous and anonymous shareholder.[1]

Turning to management, it's certainly the received wisdom that its practitioners work in the best interests of shareholders. And most of the time that's true. But there are situations where management's self-interest and that of the shareholders are at odds. To illustrate:

---

[1] These days, most managements have no idea who their shareholders are (most shares of individuals are held in a street name) except for a few large institutions.

1. With respect to compensation, management expects to be paid what the market demands (allows?) or, to put it more crassly, what it thinks it's worth. And these expectations are abetted by consulting firms who are hired by management and who understand why they've been hired. The shareholders foot the bill ultimately, of course, but that's too far down the food chain to exert much influence, at least in the short run.

2. Consider a takeover bid. Down deep, though it's usually unstated, the target firm's management often prefers the comfort of the status quo and the perks, power, prestige and compensation which go with it. Management may pay lip service to selling the company but usually only at a price which is unlikely to be available and on conditions which are unlikely to be acceptable.[2] On the other hand, from a shareholder perspective, the price and conditions offered may be attractive.

3. Take this a step further. Faced with an attractive offer, the board, representing in this situation the best interests of the shareholders, decides to sell. In anticipation of this eventuality, management will earlier have negotiated suitable downside protection for itself. Sometimes this protection would be triggered by change of control, independent of any actual change in status for an executive. This kind of aggressive golden parachute is sometimes described indelicately

---

[2] This is less likely if the CEO and many of his senior managers are themselves significant shareholders and old enough to weigh favourably the beckoning benefits of retirement against continued participation in the corporate maelstrom.

as the golden condom. It protects the user while screwing the shareholder.

4. One way for management to fend off unwanted suitors is with a shareholder rights plan. To be fair about it, a vanilla plan—that is, one which simply provides a board and management with additional time, beyond what's mandated by government regulations, to find another buyer at a higher price—should be and usually is acceptable to shareholders who have the last word in this matter.

   But plans which make a company less attractive to a buyer are, of course, anathema to shareholders. This includes such provisions as the acceleration of options, the payment of over-generous severance payments to essential executives, and the hasty sale of divisions or subsidiaries so that what remains is not what the buyer sought to acquire.

These four examples depict management self-interest at odds with legitimate shareholder interests. My final example is different. It's where management tries to steer a longer-run strategic course which is in the best interests of the enterprise but runs afoul of a short-run shareholder perspective. This is often aggravated by pension funds which, as noted earlier, often demand first-or second-quartile performance from investment managers annually or even each quarter. It's hardly a secret that many managements are frustrated and deterred from making sound longer-run strategic investments which have negative front-end and short-run impact. They blame the myopia of too many investors in the frenzied stock market environment of recent years.

Some, but certainly not all, of these examples of dissonance between management and shareholders can be alleviated, though not eliminated, by changing the mix of fixed to variable compensation in favour of the latter.

Now let's look at the board, which, on the whole, is better able than management to represent shareholder interests. This is partly because the board is, in a sense, a middleman or mediator between management and shareholders. It is also because the board has fewer conflicts of interest. For example, board fees, while admittedly considerably more generous than a decade ago, are almost never sufficient to sway a director's judgement about what's best for the shareholder.

Perhaps an occasional non-executive board chairman with a strong personality, a large stipend and a high regard for the prestige of his office might try to marshal opposition to a take-over bid which is in shareholder interests, but that would be unusual.

In fact, what's normal is a close and symbiotic relationship between board and shareholder. And, as with management, directors who receive a higher percentage of their compensation in stock options or grants and less in cash are even more likely to align themselves with shareholders.

This brings us to the shareholder whose objective is clear and simple: total shareholder return (TSR), the sum of capital gains and dividends. Any trade-off in favour of jam tomorrow rather than jam today must be justified, taking into account the time-value of shareholder capital.

Incidentally, I exclude from this comment controlling shareholders, who sometimes take both a longer and a less rigorously analytical view. This is especially likely with third- or fourth- generation shareholders in family-controlled companies who may throw into the mix a little paternalism and pride of heritage.

So much for background. Let's turn now to making some distinctions among classes of investors. This will help us to assess better the central question of whether growing shareholder influence is, on balance, a good thing or not.

It's clear that the ownership of North American corporations is increasingly concentrated through institutional investors. Over three-quarters of the shares of the S&P 500 companies are now held by institutions, a massive trend which has been building over the past couple of decades.

This is happening in Canada as well, though it's complicated by the additional phenomenon of the controlling shareholder, often a foreign parent. This is far more common on the TSE than on the NYSE.

The two largest categories by far of institutional investment are pension funds and mutual funds. The former, while overseen by trustees, are managed by professionals, sometimes in-house but, more commonly, externally.

Investments of the larger public pension funds—and they constitute, collectively, huge pools of capital—tend to be managed internally. They include funds like the Caisse, OMERS, Ontario Teachers, Ontario Hospital. Most corporate pension funds are managed externally. An exception is firms in the financial services industry which, for obvious reasons, tend to manage internally.

The external investment managers of corporate pension funds tend to defer to their clients on governance issues affecting the companies in which they invest. Clients also tend to be passive and support generally the position put forward by the company in which the pension fund is a shareholder. Perhaps this is a commercial variant of the golden rule: do unto others as you would have them do unto you. Or in modern parlance, you might be next!

With public pension funds and especially with the larger ones, the level of proactivity is high and rising. The Ontario Teachers' Plan, for example, takes a lively interest in and often strong position on a wide range of contemporary governance and other corporate issues.[3] On compensation matters alone, OTP management advocates quite strongly that corporate executives buy, with their own money, shares in their company, that the balance of their compensation be tilted away from fixed salary and towards variable compensation and, within variable, more towards stock grants and options.

A similar position is taken with directors who are admonished to buy and hold shares with their own money, to invest in shares to the tune of at least two to three times the amount of their annual retainer, and to be paid more in shares than in cash, even to the extent of foregoing cash compensation altogether.

---

3 Occasionally, some investors become concerned with broader issues, such as Talisman Energy's operations in Sudan or Nike's work practices in third-world countries or McDonald's alleged damage to the Amazonian rainforest.

I can say "occasionally" because criticism of such practices is far more likely to come from non-governmental organizations (NGOs) and other concerned constituencies and individuals than from shareholders. With few exceptions, shareholders qua shareholders are concerned only with dividends and capital gains.

Those who worry about these broader, societal issues are better-advised to buy ethical funds. However, this does not prevent a few individuals and representatives of various constituencies from buying a few shares to give them the right to make impassioned speeches at (and occasionally to disrupt), annual meetings. Call it corporate democracy.

Now a word or two about mutual funds, where prodigious amounts of money have been invested in the past ten years. Pension funds themselves often invest in mutual funds, usually in segregated form. On the whole, mutual fund managers are more passive than public pension fund managers, tending to vote with the management of corporations in which they own stock. There are, however, some notable exceptions where a few high-profile mutual fund managers speak out forcefully. I predict that this trend will intensify. The old approach, if you disagreed with some governance issue, was simply to sell the shares, the old "vote with your feet" approach. Not anymore.

It is clear that the most aggressive and outspoken protagonists for shareholder rights are the internal managers of public pension plans and the managers of mutual funds. But individual investors also have views and sometimes take to the barricades to promote them. This is illustrated in the case of the ubiquitous Mr. Michaud who, after buying a few shares in Canada's largest financial institution, the Royal Bank, was successful in getting four controversial governance issues onto shareholders ballots.

Although all four resolutions were defeated, Mr. Michaud and his supporters attracted a lot of media attention to some important governance questions like separation of the roles of board chairman and CEO, keeping related parties off boards, and limiting CEO compensation to some multiple of the pay of people at the bottom of the corporate totem pole.

The final question I want to raise is this. If there is a trend to greater shareholder influence over a wider range of corporate governance issues (and the trend is unmistakable), is this a good thing or not?

From the perspectives of society as a whole as well as of good corporate governance, the answer is a resounding yes. But there are, as usual, a couple of caveats.

First, we should remember that the institutional investor is an agent of and surrogate for the shareholder but he is not the shareholder per se. It is true that the managers of a pension fund or of a mutual fund or of the wealth of a high net-worth individual will almost always have the best interests of the shareholder in mind.

However, there is obviously potential for conflict on the subject of the level of fees which shareholders pay to have their money managed. Marketing fees, distribution fees, management fees, transaction fees, all come out of shareholder hides.

In addition, are we always certain that investment managers have done their homework and reached the right conclusions in representing shareholder interests on every issue? I have seen, for example, quite reasonable and benign shareholder rights plans attacked and even defeated on the basis of little more than whim or some generalised bias unsupported by fact. Surprisingly, even so-called vanilla plans, which seek nothing more than to give the board and management additional time to find a buyer or buyers willing to pay a higher price, have been defeated. The reason? A majority of shareholders were endemically suspicious that management was somehow entrenching itself.

But aside from such cavils, my only general concern about the growing power of shareholders, when exercised through their agents and intermediaries, is this. While the public good is, for the most part, served by these groups who set themselves up as watchdogs over potential or actual abuses of corporate power, it begs such questions as "Who will watch the watchdogs?" and "Who will ensure that one set of potential abuses is not replaced by another?"

Some argue that a second line of defence is best provided by some branch of government. Perhaps. But it runs counter to current trends to self-government, something which most of us support on principle. Part of a better answer may be public disclosure and scrutiny. It needs to be reinforced and even strengthened in some areas.

Another important part of the solution is to improve the selection, orientation, and ongoing training of the directors or trustees of pension plans, especially of public sector pension plans. Why do I make this last distinction?

In the private sector, it is common for a committee of the board to provide a comprehensive, ongoing overview of the company's pension plan, often in considerable detail. At present and in the recent past, the process for appointing directors to corporations with listed shares has been generally thorough, even exhaustive. The outcome, for the most part, is experienced, savvy, well-educated, well-trained individuals joining boards. And this means that the overseeing of the pension plan is usually carried out satisfactorily.

This was not necessarily as true a couple of decades ago, when the oft-cited old boys' network and the cosy club approach flourished. But it's almost universally true today when rigorous and demanding standards of governance at least for public companies, are the norm, motivated by dissatisfied shareholders, regulators, stock exchanges, and informed observers.

However, some public sector pension plans have not yet completed this transition from amateurism to professionalism. While many such plans, perhaps most of them, are managed professionally, their boards are too often over-stocked with persons whose principal merit is that they are members and beneficiaries of their company's pension plan and that they have been elected by their fellow employees.

While this is laudably democratic, it does not always produce the quality of direction and oversight which is essential in today's bewildering, complex, and unpredictable world.

It is both crucial and obvious that any criticism of corporate performance by shareholders and their advisors and surrogates should be informed, even-handed and far-sighted. So part of the answer consists of better-selected, better-oriented, and, on a continuing basis, better-trained pension fund trustees. More open scrutiny of the director selection and training process will help. So will more public attention paid to who sits on the boards of large public sector pension funds.

The shareholder is the ultimate beneficiary of the careful overview and, where appropriate, criticism of the actions of corporations. And so any informed individual or group wanting to take on this role and whose objectives align closely, though not perfectly, with those of shareholders, is performing a useful and even valuable service.

That may place a burr under a few saddles but should nevertheless be encouraged and welcomed.

CHAPTER 13

Some Contemporary Board Issues: Hostile Takeovers

This section on the complex and litigious subject of hostile takeovers was written five years ago, though edited very recently. As a consequence, the specific cases cited are somewhat dated. However, the issues raised by these cases and the principles discussed are much more enduring so I have not, therefore, replaced them. I must also emphasise that the viewpoints expressed represent the perspective of a businessperson, not a lawyer.

Let me begin by asking a pivotal question: Once a hostile bid has been made, who decides acceptance or rejection—the board or the shareholders? One has the knowledge; the others have the power of the vote. Is any bid price which is comfortably above the pre-bid market price sufficient? Or can management argue that, with its in-depth knowledge of future plans, the shares will appreciate even more if management is left to carry on and implement those plans?

Often disagreement centres on short-run versus longer-run value. Net present value calculations are, of course, intended to adjust for varying time frames. But, since the future is inherently unpredictable, the calculations are subject to many assumptions and wide swings and, therefore, to disagreement and to error.

In many attempted hostile takeovers, the issue goes far beyond differences in value over time. Such qualitative factors as pride, anger, and covetousness often play central roles. In fact, the only one of the seven deadly sins not normally involved is sloth.

The public contretemps between Service Corp. International and the Loewen Group of a few years ago is instructive. After SCI bid U.S.$43, Ray Loewen was quoted as saying that "U.S.$50, U.S.$52, would not put any pressure on me."

In short, much more than price is involved. Blending the management styles of the world's two largest funeral home operators would be, as Mr. Loewen was quoted as saying, like trying to mix water and oil. He noted that SCI was attempting to eliminate a competitor which "has out-competed and outhustled" SCI. That sounds more like pride and anger than mere dollars and cents.

In terms of outcomes, there are examples on all sides of the issue. A dozen years ago, Paramount tried to buy Time Warner for U.S.$50 a share, adjusted for a subsequent 4 for 1 stock split. The Time Warner board rejected the offer. Seven years later, Time Warner stock was still languishing at $39.50 a share. Shareholders had left U.S.$4 billion on the table.

By contrast, the board of Puritan-Bennett in the U.S. turned down a $24.50 bid by Thermo-Electron when the market price was $20. A year later, it accepted an offer of $36 from Nellcor. A good delaying decision, a good eventual outcome.

Then there are cases where shareholders have voted and have proven to be wrong, at least in the short run. In 1995, the shareholders of Hills Stores in the U.S. voted for a change of control and of management. The cost of this change, including expensive golden parachutes, reduced the value of the stock by about U.S.$4 per share, a loss which took years to recoup.

In Europe, more fundamental questions are raised. In Germany, Volkswagen and some other companies have begun to express doubts whether a policy of maximising financial return is reconcilable with consensus-based industrial relations. Volkswagen management has said openly that "workholder value" should carry equal weight with "shareholder value." That view would, of course, be unacceptable in current North American management and financial thinking.

A less controversial but nevertheless leading-edge view has been expressed by Jürgen Schrempp, now chairman of the Daimler-Chrylser group. While he remains an "energetic advocate of shareholder value," he distinguishes between short-term opportunistic dealing and the building of long-term value. "Shareholder value must not be pushed for short-term success at the expense of future viability and future earnings potential."

Many North American corporate executives would support this sentiment but this considerable scepticism in German boardrooms about shareholder value in the immediate sense is not much shared in North American financial markets.

To show the wide range of views in North America, consider these two extremes. On the one hand, a bylaw proposed by a dissident shareholder of Wallace Computer Services, which rejected a takeover bid by Moore Corporation, would require Wallace to hold a shareholder vote on the company's defence strategy, given a fully financed offer at a price 25% above the pre-bid stock price. The Moore Corporation bid had met this condition. The takeover never did take place.

On the other hand, proposals have been bruited about for years that, in the event of a hostile takeover bid, only institutions or individuals that have held their shares for at least six months would be entitled to bid. Such proposals are obviously designed to thwart arbitrageurs who leap into the fray opportunistically looking for a quick buck. In fact, the six-month rule might even put them out of business.

Are such short-term players entitled or not to the same rights as longer-term investors? In terms of existing corporate law, the reformers haven't a leg to stand on. Within a given class, a share is a share is a share. But in terms of the best interests of society as a whole, the issue has not yet been joined in any substantive way. On the whole, I believe that a six-month rule would place more needed emphasis on strategy and less unneeded emphasis on opportunism. But I wouldn't hold my breath awaiting implementation.

SOME DIFFERENCES BETWEEN U.S. AND CANADIAN CORPORATE BOARDS

What follows are a few perceptions about some of the differences between Canadian and U.S. public-company board practice. My comments are based partly on serving on a couple of U.S. boards over the years (granted, a small sample), more on staying abreast of some of the many relevant articles written in both countries.

The biggest difference is that oft-cited one: in Canada, some two-thirds of public company boards separate the roles of chairman and CEO. In the U.S., more than two-thirds combine them.

I will not insult the reader by repeating here the standard arguments advanced in favour of separation of roles. In governance terms, these arguments are as well known as they are compelling. The most obvious consequence of role separation is that power and responsibility are divided and a creative tension is introduced into the relationship between the chairman and the board, on one hand, and the CEO and management, on the other.

In Canada, this separation is generally viewed favourably as one pillar of sound governance. In the U.S., it's more frequently regarded, at least in business circles and certainly—no surprise here—by most CEOs, as a nuisance and a hindrance to corporate performance. It is seen as giving a higher priority to process than to performance and results.

To digress for a moment, it is interesting to recall that Americans, in their choice of government structure, adopted—over 200 years ago, of course—a highly diffuse model with four separate centres of power: two autonomous branches of Congress, an administration, and a Supreme Court.

By contrast, the Canadian parliamentary system is highly centralized (ignoring federal-provincial jurisdictional issues). When a federal political party wins a plurality of seats and power, the House and the Senate are very secondary to the Cabinet on any issue which matters and, within the Cabinet, the Prime Minister is much more than *primus inter pares*. Forget the *inter pares*.

The U.S. seems to prefer government with power divided but a business structure with power more concentrated. In Canada, we seem content to have government with power concentrated but business with power more divided. On this last point, several Canadian bank chairmen might ruefully agree.

Does this make a comment about the relative importance of government and business in the two countries? One could argue that the U.S. has opted for a government structure which favours the preservation of the status quo and a corporate structure in which business is empowered to act proactively and aggressively. In Canada, some believe that at least part of the reverse is true, using the failed bank mergers to buttress their case.

But back to differences in how boards operate in the two countries. If the CEO in the U.S. is more empowered, more able to operate independently, this probably reflects in part a difference in ownership structure in the two countries. In Canadian public companies, there is often a controlling or at least a significant shareholder. In the U.S., this is less of a factor though it does, of course, exist. A controlling shareholder usually wants to make its presence felt. One way is for that shareholder to meet quietly with management on a regular basis so as to ensure that its objectives and needs are met, subject to fairness to other shareholders. Another way is to appoint a chairman who represents that large shareholder.

If it is true that the CEOs of widely held U.S. companies usually have more freedom to operate, vis-à-vis their boards, than in Canada, it's only true so long as things are going well. The record is overflowing with widely publicized cases where U.S. boards have turned against and turfed out their CEOs because of performance issues or disagreement over strategic direction. The typical U.S. board may be a paper tiger so long as sales and earnings and share prices rise at suitably aggressive rates. But the tiger is real and the claws come out when performance is poor.

In Canada, boards tend to exercise more ongoing routine constraints on management's freedom to act unilaterally. In a widely held company, these constraints are more likely to involve extra process than any genuine thwarting of the CEO's will, especially on a matter where he feels strongly and always assuming performance is acceptable or better. With a controlling shareholder, it is frequently another story, depending on several factors of which performance is one but not the only one.

Another thing. U.S. boards talk about their share prices more frankly and frequently than Canadian boards. And why not? Obviously what matters to shareholders are share prices and dividends. And, until the great reckoning which began in the second half of 2000, forget the dividends...at least with dot-com and other growth and (especially) momentum stocks. In fact, again until recently, forget even the earnings. Simply demonstrate high double-digit revenue growth, preferably actual although projected works almost as well. These violations of time-tested measures of performance could not, of course, last for long... and they didn't. God's mills take their time grinding but they get the job done.

In Canada, many boards rarely discuss share price performance. It's as if the subject is unseemly, like belching in church. What happens in the stock market is too often viewed as beyond corporate control, as an exogenous variable. That boards might consider legitimate steps to make a stock more appealing to shareholders has been played down, at least historically, much more in Canada than in the U.S.

Clearly there are limits which must be observed. If a management worries about share price appreciation to the point that it neglects operations, that's folly. And the manipulation of earnings is, of course, anathema.[1] But, subject always to the immutable constraints of integrity, transparency, and ethical standards, shareholder interests are best served if more than desultory service is paid to share price enhancement.

LIABILITIES WHERE DUE DILIGENCE IS NO DEFENSE

A few years ago, I was invited to appear before the Standing Senate Committee on Banking, Trade and Commerce to discuss possible changes to the Canada *Business Corporations Act*. The committee had asked several witnesses to

---

[1] That is, it should be anathema. But, as the Enron debacle demonstrates, "should" is prescriptive; reality can be sordid.

make statements and answer questions on a variety of corporate governance issues as its members met in half a dozen cities across Canada.

I chose to address three topics, two of which—separation of roles of chairman and CEO, and regular versus advisory boards—are covered in more depth elsewhere in this book. The third topic was flaws in legislation governing directors' and officers' statutory liabilities in certain situations where due diligence is not a defense.

An abridged version of my remarks on this subject follows:

Current legislation poses a dilemma for directors of a company facing the prospect of insolvency. If they choose to stay the course, they are exposed to personal liability, often of catastrophic proportions, for unpaid corporate taxes, back wages, and accrued vacations. And due diligence is no defense.

If, facing this potentially ruinous set of personal liabilities, a director, or sometimes an entire board, decides to resign, there is the stigma of abandoning an enterprise when its need is greatest. In at least one such real-life case, this charge was hurled at the directors: "Like rats deserting a sinking ship."

I would like to underscore the senselessness of the present legislation in most circumstances. I do not doubt that there are cases where an unscrupulous owner-manager of a small business may court bankruptcy in order to flout legitimate claims of the workforce. This is the exception and, of course, new legislation must take this into account.

cont.

More typical is the situation where honest, hard-working directors, doing everything in their power to keep the ship afloat, face an inevitable drift towards corporate insolvency. They are confronted, quite unfairly, with onerous personal liabilities and even, on occasion, with personal bankruptcy.

Any law which forces directors to resign at the very moment when they are needed most is dysfunctional in the extreme. Once I faced this situation myself and may I add that once was enough. The company was Inter-link Freight Systems. (It is discussed elsewhere in this book in a different context.) For a mix of reasons, the company's losses mounted and the spectre of corporate insolvency within a matter of months faced each of us as directors.

For historical reasons going back many decades, the company paid its almost three thousand employees retroactively to the tune of about a three-week delay, on average. That, along with accrued vacation liabilities, which built in the first half of the year and were at their greatest around the end of June, created a significant personal liability for directors in the early months of 1996.

Our best efforts, our mounting concerns, and our meeting frequency all coincided until, one fateful evening, the board met for five hours. At almost precisely midnight, the entire board (eleven persons less one who had resigned a week or so earlier) resigned.

A few moments before our collective decision, one of the directors, a well-known labour leader, had relieved the heavy tension in the air by saying, "There

cont.

are only two things I really value in life: my wife and my pick-up truck." (pause) "And I really don't want to lose my pick-up truck."

This case is a classic example of directors forced by unreasonably punitive legislation into abandoning the duty they owe to shareholders, employees, and other stakeholders.

I know that this committee is well aware of the deep flaws in the present legislation. I urge you to recommend, as forcefully as you are able, that this intolerable situation be remedied as soon as feasible.

POSTSCRIPT

That was in 1996 and it's a sad but unsurprising comment on the legislative process that progress is often so excruciatingly slow. However, finally, on November 24, 2001, Bill 5-11[2] came into force.

Among a host of other needed reforms, it entitles directors of a CBCA corporation to rely on a "due diligence" defence for a wide range of liabilities. This should go a long way to ensuring that directors, like ship captains, neither leave the ship in danger of sinking nor, to continue the nautical analogy, go down with the vessel in the sorry event it fails to stay afloat.

---

[2] An act to amend the Canada *Business Corporations Act* and the Canada *Cooperatives Act*, as well as other acts.

Some Personal Experiences as a Director (IV)

I've had the interesting (as in the apocryphal Chinese curse: may you live in interesting times) experience of sitting on sixteen boards where either the company was acquired and taken over or the company and the board ceased to function, for one reason or another. Thirteen of these were takeovers. Some were friendly, some hostile. Some were solicited, some not. In most instances, the new owners replaced the previous directors with nominees of their own. Each of the other three cases was different.

First, there was the large multinational company which concluded that the board of its 100%-owned Canadian subsidiary was complicating global strategy. It changed to an advisory board, which operated for two or three years but was then itself later eliminated. That was Monsanto Canada Limited. Its parent company, Monsanto Corporation of St. Louis, was acquired in 2000 by Pharmacia, itself the earlier merger of Pharmacia and Upjohn.

Then there was the Canadian company where the controlling shareholder bought out a substantial minority interest of long standing for essentially the same reason. That was Canadian Business Media Limited, now 100% owned by Rogers Communications Inc.

And finally there was a company which found itself in financial trouble after NAFTA changed the pattern of freight movement in Canada from predominately east-west to substantially north-south. In such a situation, directors face personal liabilities for certain corporate obligations, such as back wages and accrued vacations, where due diligence, under current CBCA rules, is no defense. As the bottom line continued to deteriorate, the directors resigned one midnight, at the end of a five-hour board meeting. The company survived without independent directors for almost another year. Then it went into bankruptcy and eventually disappeared. That was Interlink Freight Systems, mentioned earlier in this book.

So what's to be learned from these three tales? First, as is dazzlingly obvious, it's a volatile world out there. What appears to be the epitome of normality and stability today can all too easily degenerate into massive, unanticipated change tomorrow, usually accompanied by turbulence and a fair amount of anguish. Second, as if you didn't know, job security for directors today is on a par with that segment of trapeze artists who prefer to work without a net.

I mentioned that I've been a director of thirteen companies that were subsequently acquired by other corporations.

What follows is a war story which describes one of these sometimes traumatic events. In 1988, a hostile takeover bid was made for control of the Canada Development Corporation by Bob Blair, then the CEO and a large shareholder of Nova Corporation.

The CDC, as you may recall, was created by the Canadian government as a hybrid company and as something of an experiment. It opened its doors for business in 1971. It would operate in the private sector for profit but would also be expected to meet certain broad public policy objectives, like injecting a Canadian presence into various industry sectors. This two-part mission eventually proved impossible to fulfill in a predominately free-enterprise business milieu.

But back to the Blair takeover bid. Eventually, a special meeting of shareholders was called. Noranda Inc., a significant shareholder, voted originally against the takeover. However, on the morning of the special meeting, they changed their proxy and voted to support the bid.

When the final vote was tabulated, the results were so close that the Noranda switch made the difference. The CDC board chairman and the chairman of that day's special meeting was Pierre Coté, a highly experienced multi-company director from Quebec. After hurried consultation with a phalanx of legal advisors and with his board, of which I was a member, he concluded that the Noranda proxy change had arrived too late to count.

The issue was sufficiently ambiguous that the lawyers were divided but the chairman went with those who counselled that the proxy change was invalid. After considerable delay, he announced that the takeover bid was defeated. When there is reasonable doubt, go for the best outcome.

The meeting lasted for something like ten hours, count-ing a couple of long recesses for regrouping. The decision to reject was not, of course, greeted with universal approval, given the CDC's mediocre performance record.

Not surprisingly, Mr. Blair forced another vote a few weeks later. This time he succeeded in gaining control. Since the CDC was a highly diversified conglomerate oper-ating in a lot of unrelated sectors, Mr. Blair's plan from the beginning and the one he implemented was to keep the businesses which seemed to him to be compatible with Nova's various businesses and either to sell or shut down the rest. As a result, the CDC was dismantled.

As a matter of fact, it was dismantled even more com-pletely than Mr. Blair had planned. A year or so earlier, the leadership of the CDC had passed from Tony Hampson, who had been CEO for fifteen years—pretty much from the beginning—to Bernard Isautier, a Frenchman from Paris. Mr. Isautier was a tough, shrewd bargainer and, throughout the negotiations, the ante was raised several times. A year or so before Mr. Blair entered the picture, the CDC stock was selling at around $7 a share. The actual price achieved, including a special dividend paid, was about $33 a share. As a consequence, Mr. Blair was pressed into selling more of what he acquired than he had planned on.

For ten years, I had chaired the board of a major CDC subsidiary, Polysar Chemical Company. Polysar was a suc-cessful, profitable, research-intensive company formed as a Crown Corporation during WWII to produce synthetic rubber after Japan had taken control of Malaysia's natural rubber plantations. Everyone connected with Polysar was proud of both its heritage and its ongoing success. As a result of the takeover of the CDC, Polysar was broken up. Many of its key people either retired or went on to other things.

I think it's fair to say that there was some bitterness, certainly in the executive ranks, that Polysar was caught up in a wider struggle. I have always believed that it deserved better. Having said that, the CDC shareholders were well pleased with the broader outcome.

And what can we learn from this? Certainly it's well known, almost axiomatic, that few mergers are successful from the viewpoint of the shareholders of both the acquiring and the acquired companies. And it's always unfortunate when a viable component of a parent with indifferent results gets sideswiped in a takeover and disappears. That's what happened to Polysar and that is why it no longer appears, as it did for many years, on the back of Canada's ten-dollar bill.

CHAPTER 14

Three Core Principles of Effective Corporate Governance

I should like to end this book by recapitulating and expanding on remarks I made at a Fellowship Awards Dinner sponsored by the Institute of Corporate Directors and held on April 29, 1999. In a recent reread of what I said that evening, I began to have some concern that the three bedrock principles of sound corporate governance which I tried to articulate may, to some readers, come across as somewhat obvious and perhaps even simplistic. Yet each of them is ignored or violated often enough that reiteration of some basics may be helpful and a gentle reminder that what is obvious to Jack and Jill may be anything but to Jim and Jane. So here they are.

Twenty years ago, governance was at a rather primitive level of development. It needed considerable attention and change. And during these past twenty years, it has indeed received much attention and change. Along with many others, I'm glad to have played a small part in this vitalization. I use the word "vitalization," because revitalization implies a return to *former* vitality—not, on this topic, a very defensible proposition.

Over the years, I've come to realize that corporate governance often means different things to different people. Lack of a common understanding can cause problems. My understanding of what good corporate governance means can be captured in three propositions, none of which are breathtakingly original.

• First, a board should not, must not, indeed cannot manage. When it tries to do so, as it does from time to time, it's no longer a board. It has become a management. And in such a circumstance, I'm reminded of Samuel Johnson's oft-quoted remark in a different context: "It is like a dog walking on his hind legs. It is not done well but you are surprised to find it done at all."

Why would a board move into management in the first place? The reasons are varied. Sometimes it's the combination of a dominant non-executive chairman—perhaps a former CEO—and a new and at least temporarily insecure CEO. Perhaps it's the presence on the board of one or more large shareholders who are aggressive or impatient or both. Or perhaps it's because of a temporary and unplanned absence of full-time leadership, such as when a CEO resigns, is fired, or is hit by a lorry, as an English colleague likes to put it.

The hazards which inevitably accompany the phenomenon of a board trying to manage, even when forced by circumstances and when the intention is to find a full-time new CEO post haste, are predictable and serious.

Damage to morale in the management ranks is common and is often accompanied by a "we and they" mindset. Problems can also arise through insufficient knowledge or experience or even availability of time on the part of the protem CEO or the board as a whole, which finds itself playing a more proactive role than it is accustomed to playing.

Still another problem can arise when a retired member of management regains power, despite being out of touch and perhaps dated. Or perhaps a non-executive chair, who is not a previous CEO of the company, is thrust into the CEO role, even if only temporarily, often without fully appropriate background and knowledge and perhaps with other commitments which impede single-minded devotion to the looming task at hand.

All of this suggests that a board should stay out of management, except when dictated by unforeseen circumstances and only for as short a time as possible. And even then, its highest priority must be to find a new CEO and to revert to doing what it should be doing: to provide wise counsel and oversight and to work collaboratively with management in the best interests of shareholders.

• Second, there surely is a legitimate and indeed essential role for boards. This may seem blindingly obvious except that we have all run across cranks and cynics who think that corporations would function better without boards. They are convinced that directors do not make a difference and have little impact on society. I beg to differ. In

a democracy, everyone must be accountable to someone. In a dictatorship, this principle is renounced and I
need hardly remind you of the consequences.

Still, there are observers—and not all of them are
cranks and cynics—who continue to feel that boards are
superfluous. It's important to understand why. I'm convinced that the most common and understandable reason
is the failure of a fair number of boards—a small minority,
granted, but still too many—to prevent excesses and even
disasters. These include disastrous investments, fraud,
excessive management compensation, entrenchment of
management rights, and—the ultimate failure—bankruptcy.

But these are failures, not of board governance as a
principle, but of specific examples of the practice of board
governance. The great majority of boards provide valuable
oversight of a kind which, if boards did not exist, would
have to be invented. When discussing boards, this must
always be kept in mind. Oversight and judgement are what
boards are truly about and why good governance matters.

Having said that, I do not want to imply that all procedure is meaningless and irrelevant. In that direction lies
confusion and even anarchy. But procedural matters need
to be kept in perspective and in check. They need to be
balanced continuously against the much higher priority of
substantive accomplishment. This means measurable
results which must translate eventually and preferably
sooner into higher returns—some mix of capital gains and
dividends—to shareholders.

In theory, management could report to the shareholders directly and solely, without intermediation. But at least
in publicly traded companies with many shareholders, any

direct link between management and shareholders is, as academics like to phrase it, necessary but insufficient. That is, shareholders are too diffuse and amorphous a group to be reported to exclusively in this way, except superficially. The kind of direct management-to-shareholder reporting that takes place via quarterly and annual reports and face to face meetings with investors, while important, is not enough.

And so boards of directors, once little more than cheering sections for management, but now mostly comprising independent men and women, fill a crucial gap. They have become an essential intermediary between management and shareholders.

While the goals of management and shareholders are, for the most part, congruent, there are exceptions (such as executive compensation, where the board plays the important role of balancing the inevitable presence of managerial self-interest with the realities of supply and demand for talent). This particular role, incidentally, is more exquisitely difficult to perform well than it might superficially appear. Not the least of the potential snares and traps is the co-optation of one set of players by another.

Boards themselves face similar conflicts, of course, in relation to their own compensation. However, some would argue that directors' fees, certainly in Canada, are usually modest enough that any conflict in theory is *de minimis* in practice.

• My third and final proposition is to re-emphasize that it is important for both directors and management never, ever to be overly consumed by or even concerned with process. Rather they must focus on results. Whenever governance puts process ahead of performance, it has gone too far. It has forgotten the name of the game.

What I mean by this is that, subject to the law, ethical behavior, and long-term sustainability, what is accomplished and what eventually is displayed on a balance sheet or at the bottom of an income statement are what truly matters. They are obviously more important than focusing obsessively on the minutiae and adhering in slavish detail to a three-volume procedures manual.

In recent years, I have observed a growing rift between some CEOs and other senior executives, on the one hand, and some advocates of more aggressive corporate governance, on the other.

There are CEOs who fear that too much concern for process will kill or at least wound the proverbial golden goose. I share this fear. However, there are other CEOs and executives who go several steps further and view modern corporate governance as an invasion of turf and as a threat to their role and their authority. Here I do not agree.

At the same time, I also disagree with those observers of the corporate scene and shareholder activists and academics and media gurus who believe that, despite the massive progress made over the past decade or so, the role of the board still needs to be strengthened dramatically. Revolution, not evolution. If the truth were known, some commentators seem to want management to be little more than the board's servant. *De facto*, the board becomes the employer and management becomes the employee. In this zeitgeist, the CEO reports to the board chairman in every meaningful sense of the word "report." This is both inappropriate and entirely unworkable.

The relationship between a chair and a CEO is not even remotely like that between, say, a president and a vice-president. Neither is it like the relationship between two golfing or fishing buddies. My view is simple. The very best boards (and I've been involved over the years with several of these) recognize that the primary roles of the board and management are different and that it is crucial that they not be confused. When they overlap, as inevitably they will from time to time, this is dealt with responsibly. The key is mutual respect and maturity. Ideally, there is at work a common dedication to a single set of goals of which the best measure by far is total shareholder return sustained over long periods. But there is also a recognition that there are various sorts of responsibilities to or constraints imposed by other stakeholders as well.

Here's my cursory appraisal of where we're at today in the evolution of corporate governance. In my view, the best companies—perhaps the top 10% or 15%—are close to an acceptable, even ideal, state for the foreseeable future. There's fine-tuning needed here and there but nothing major. The big challenge is to close the considerable gap between the best and the rest.

For smaller companies, the cost of maintaining a sound governance regimen must be taken into account. But this does not relieve them of their responsibilities. Striking the balance between deficiency and cost will require a healthy dollop of ingenuity and flexibility. As an inveterate optimist, I believe that this challenge will be met successfully.

Despite a large claque of cynics, naysayers and doomsayers, the chronically pessimistic, the underinformed, and inveterate pundits of many stripes, corporate governance is alive and well and serving the economy and society reasonably well, all-in, in most developed countries, including our own.

Does this mean that further improvements are unnecessary or impossible? Of course not.

Does it mean that there will be no more cases where companies have failed (the list is too long for comfort) and where strong, alert, experienced boards could have, might have made the difference? Sadly, no.

Does it mean that incompetent executives and inept directors are banished from the face of the earth and that no managements or boards will ever again be culpable for a litany of sins and shortcomings, ranging through insularity, inexperience, inaction and indecisiveness, short-sightedness, pig-headedness, reckless and impetuous decision-making, and rampant greed? The list could be extended but, in any event, the answer again is no.

And, finally, does it mean that outright dishonesty will be barred from executive suites and boardrooms so that cardinal sins like fraud and deception will never again darken corporate doors? Sadly and in a word: no.

So what does it mean? It means that most boards of most companies most of the time provide and will continue to provide value. They help to enhance performance. And if these boards did not exist, that performance would, on average, be worse than it is and boards would, as I said earlier, have to be reinvented.

Perhaps this is too modest a claim. Let me rephrase it. While all boards can do better, most do well. Fine-tuning may sound like an avoidance of larger issues but it's not. For most organizations, it's all that's needed on a continuing basis.

I can do no better than end by observing that what Winston Churchill said about democracy is equally applicable to modern-day corporate governance: "No one pretends that democracy is perfect or all-wise. Indeed, it has been said that democracy is the worst form of government except all those other forms that have been tried from time to time."

Public Company Director Accreditation[1]

Should directors of public companies—those with listed shares—be formally accredited? A generation ago, the question was unlikely to be asked. If it had been, it would almost certainly have been answered in the negative by most informed observers.

But times have changed. The role of the director today is more onerous and demanding, more complex and multi-dimensional. There are more risks; potential liabilities are heavy. Society expects and demands more from directors; compensation has risen in response. In sum, the director's role has become more, well, professional. And it is quite

---

[1] From *Ivey Business Quarterly*, Winter 1998.

likely that, if we look forward a decade, the increase in the knowledge and skills required of directors will be as dramatic as the anticipated level of change in the environment in which business operates.

Recent situations where boards have failed to protect shareholders against fraud, mismanagement or just plain incompetence are unsettling. Bre-X is a much-publicized example of a long list of situations where shareholders ask pointedly whether boards and managements have failed and why.

Many, indeed most, companies today operate in increasingly competitive or even hostile environments where survival, let alone success, depends heavily on the combined skills of an effective management team and of a board which oversees judiciously and with foresight.

The issue of accreditation is, of course, a long-settled matter for accountants, actuaries, architects, dentists, engineers, physicians, and sales representatives in a wide range of fields including insurance, real estate, and securities. A complete list would be still longer.

Some of these occupations are called professions; some perhaps are not, at least in the traditional sense, although distinctions are increasingly blurred in a knowledge-based world and one in which accountability is both crucial and universal.

If at least professions should be formally accredited, what are the relevant criteria for defining a profession in the context of directorship? Here are three:

1. Is there a body of knowledge and a discipline which directors must understand and master in order to carry out their responsibilities fully and properly?

2. Is there an essential bond of trust between directors and one or more stakeholders including, of course, shareholders?

3. Do directors as a class impact in a significant way on the welfare of society as a whole?

Twenty or thirty years ago, I would have answered these three questions like this:

1. Not really.

2. Yes, though sometimes more *de jure* than *de facto*.

3. Doubtful.

But today the answer in each case is, I believe, strongly affirmative.

What would accreditation entail? At a summary level, the following points may be useful:

- There would be an entry-level test which would examine candidates on all important aspects of directorship. These would include such obvious categories as relevant securities law; significant accounting conventions and policies; when and how directors are exposed to and protected against lawsuits; the respective roles of the chairman, the chief executive officer, the corporate secretary and general counsel, and various board committees; the range of compensation mixes for both senior management and directors; good practices (e.g., holding shares until retirement); bad practices (e.g., re-pricing options). And these few categories only scratch the surface. Directorship excellence involves much more than legal and accounting rules and conventions, important though these are. And while there is no substitute for experience, some of the less tangible, more qualitative aspects can be communicated effectively through education and feedback through testing.

I should add that in-company training, while necessary and important, should be viewed as a supplement to and not a substitute for a broader kind of training which emphasizes best practice at a national and even international level.

- There would be a small, permanent secretariat to administer the accreditation process (which would, of course, be self-regulating). It goes without saying that self-regulation is unequivocally critical to widespread acceptance of any accreditation process, including the entry examination, admission to and continuing membership in the profession, and an appropriate disciplinary process. Members would pay an annual fee to cover related costs.

- There would also be a continuing education component involving not only preparation for the entry test but ongoing program and course offerings in more specialialized or advanced aspects of directorship. This would involve seasoned directors and specialists as lecturers, panelists, authors, etc.

- After successful completion of the entry examination and after also serving for no less than, say, three years on the board of a publicly listed company, an appropriate designation would be conferred. This might be Ch.Dir. (chartered director) or something akin.

- The rudiments of an accreditation model should not be difficult to convert into a working process. The precedent of a wide range of professions is there for all to see.

As always, the devil is in the details. If and when the principle of accreditation is widely supported, a task force could likely produce a working model within six to twelve months. Under whose auspices? Who has a strong, continuing interest in ensuring that directors operate at the highest level of professionalism?

An alliance of several organizations might best fit the bill, such as the Toronto Stock Exchange, the Institute of Corporate Directors, and institutional representatives of other professions—accounting and law come to mind though others could be equally helpful—with experience in what does and doesn't work in a professional organization and with a lively interest in raising directorship standards.

An aspect which is worth further analysis is the state of play in other jurisdictions. It appears, for example, in Australia that voluntary accreditation is available with a diploma for taking a basic course and passing a test, and with a designation—AICD Fellow—for those who, having passed the test, serve on a public company board for at least five years.

What are the most plausible objections to director accreditation or at least which are most likely to be raised? Included on any list are probably some of these:

- Directorship is not a profession any more than being a CEO is a profession. We don't accredit CEOs; they earn their spurs by performance on the job.

    Executives and managers and, yes, directors have occupations, not professions. It would be too limiting to saddle directors with the trappings and obligations which accompany a profession.

- It is demeaning to think of directors in terms of licensing—for that's what accreditation is really a euphemism for. Most directors, usually senior members of the business community and often of society more broadly, will find this sort of regimentation and conformity too binding, even offensive.

- Our economic and business system works fine now, without the added complications and red tape and regulations of a licensing regime. If it ain't broke....

- Even though any director accreditation process would operate completely within the private sector, it would be only a step removed from government intervention and even control. It might tempt government at some level to want to get involved or even to take over the process. If you don't provide the tent, the camel can't put his head inside it. (In dissenting from this last observation, a colleague of mine noted that government is quite capable of providing both the tent and the camel.)

- There are already enough risks and uncertainties, difficulties and pitfalls, with being a director today. The all-in reward/risk profile is not particularly attractive. The compensation per hour is less, sometimes considerably less, than that paid to investment bankers, senior counsel, and CEOs. By superimposing another stratum of complication, the net calculus of directorship deteriorates further. Is the game worth the candle?

    More specifically, would there be sufficient added value either to society or to directors themselves who would need to prepare for and pass an examination, be accredited, be permitted to use a designation, be subject to a disciplinary process for those who betray a

trust, pay an annual fee, and be expected through continuing education to stay permanently abreast of relevant developments? To put it another way, would the
added process, cost, and nuisance-value be justified by
the prospects of improved directorship performance?

- And as a friend of mine recently told me, "I don't want
to sit on ten boards and become a so-called professional
director. As CEO of a public company, I just want to sit
on my own board without having to go through a rigmarole of unnecessary complication. Is that too much to
ask?"

Some time ago, I circulated an earlier draft of this article
to a dozen and a half persons with considerable experience in governance matters and whose views I respect.

Most of them believe that director accreditation is far
less likely to be supported and to happen if the process is
mandatory and universal, i.e., imposed on directors. Only
a few support mandatory accreditation, especially if an
attempt were made to impose it from the start.

Some feel a two-stage approach might work. In stage
one, the process would be entirely voluntary. Training,
testing, and accreditation would be available to but not
required of either existing or new directors. After a suitable period of, say, five years, the voluntary process in
place would be evaluated carefully and the pros and cons
of moving to mandatory accreditation would be weighed
even more carefully.

It is, I think, obvious that mandatory accreditation
would imply some body with sufficient authority to
impose it. Could any private-sector group or alliance of
groups ever marshal the necessary resolve to accomplish

this? If not would the spectre of a government-administered system frighten off even those in favour of universal director accreditation?

And even if these two formidable hurdles—accepting the principle of mandatory accreditation and agreeing on who would manage the process—could be surmounted, several thorny side-issues would need to be considered, including:

- Would existing directors be granted a generous grace period before having to be accredited?

- Would highly experienced directors be granted the designation without testing?

- Alternatively, would grandfathering be allowed in which existing directors would neither be required to go through the process nor be granted the designation? In some circumstances, this might be politically necessary to obtain broad support for the concept. But full implementation would obviously be delayed.

Despite these concerns and cavils, qualms and quibbles, which can, to some degree, be alleviated by keeping the accreditation process as straightforward and unadorned as possible, I believe that the benefits of accreditation—especially voluntary accreditation—outweigh the negatives. It would help all directors but new ones in particular to do their jobs better and with a surer sense of protection against at least some of the pitfalls.

It does not, of course, guarantee competency and implies nothing about judgement. But the fact that a new process fails to solve all problems is insufficient reason to reject it. In an era of increasing demands on directors, any improvement in qualifications and any consequent improvement in performance (even marginal), are surely welcome.

In response then to the question raised in the very first sentence of this article—should directors of public companies be formally accredited?—my considered if personal response is a guarded yes. A generation ago, I would have said absolutely not. And since the role of the director continues to evolve, is still in some ways a work in progress, today's guarded yes could soon become an unqualified yes.

Is it too early? Perhaps. But it is not, I submit, too early to begin an informed debate.

SUMMARY

As several people pointed out to me, the ultimate test of accreditation of any kind is whether it leads to improved corporate performance. Some were hopeful; a lesser number were sceptical.

Many felt (and I agree) that not many corporate failures or frauds would be averted as a result of accreditation. That's asking too much; it's not a panacea.

On the other hand, it is likely that, to the extent good directorship matters (if it doesn't, the whole concept of corporate governance is a mockery), corporate performance would, on average and at the margin, be improved. Because we're dealing with a complex, multi-variable relationship, no one will ever know for certain. Nevertheless, the central thrust of this article is that, based on a rough mix of reason and intuition, director accreditation would make a positive difference.

Finally, a number of my respondents were interested in next steps. While this is a reasonable area of enquiry, my feeling is that, until the principle of director accreditation has been exposed to and supported by a broader audience, it is premature to discuss implementation beyond the preliminary thoughts broached in this article.

SUMMARY OF
COMMENTS ON ARTICLE

In preparing my paper on director accreditation, I sent an earlier draft to a dozen and a half distinguished persons with considerable and varied experience in senior management, in corporate governance and directorship, and in regulation and the law.

Here are a representative cross-section of responses to my request for comments.

- I think there is a significant undercurrent of disenchantment with the corporate world, with the "monied world," and with those in authority.

  So what am I leading to? I think you're on the right horse... people will be looking increasingly to those in charge of the community's capital plant to justify why, and the manner in which, they hold the reins.

- Isn't the idea of director accreditation an infringement on the fundamental principle that the owners of a business—that is, the shareholders—should be able to elect whomever they want to the corporation's board of directors?

If they want to elect Bozo the Clown or Kermit the Frog, why should regulatory authorities intervene and require that all directors have certain minimum credentials?

- Because being a corporate director is well and truly a human endeavour, the capacity to apply judgement with wisdom, courage, etc., goes to the heart of the issue. These are matters that can't so much be tested or learned and a real assessment of the extent to which an individual may possess these capacities might be too much for the accreditation process to bear—yet they are all-important.

- I think it is important to emphasize the self-regulatory aspect of such an initiative.

- People will warm to the idea if the future can be shown to be non-threatening. This can be achieved successfully for the "old guard" by emphasizing grandfathering.

- In this age, where there is a greater need for diversity among directors, accreditation probably becomes more important. I would not be against accreditation if it started on a volunteer basis for everyone who wanted to be accredited; however, I believe that the best regulator of directors is the market. I think your idea is provocative and worthy of further debate but you can see that I come out on the side of market regulation.

- I think your paper is thought-provoking and on point with my own view of the radar screen on corporate governance issues.

- It is certainly an interesting proposition and one that may be yet another element in the continuing evolution of corporate governance disciplines.

- I agree that director accreditation would be desirable but I am not sure that it can be forced.

- While I agree that the growing realization of the need for good governance demands a more professional approach to directorship, I am not persuaded that formal accreditation is warranted.

- I am instinctively in accord with the direction of your views, particularly with the growing responsibility and "public face" of directors of public companies. An accreditation process with a credible designation could add value to professionalism in the role of corporate directors.

- With formal accreditation, I fear a new level of bureaucracy and process that would discourage good candidates.

- The qualifications are varied and I do not believe can be categorized under any accreditation process.

- With formal accreditation, people will know the horse that they're buying.
  A country with formal accreditation—especially if other countries don't have it—could gain a competitive advantage.

- I don't think accreditation would make much difference in performance—certainly not enough to justify the costs—and it would have the downside that it might prevent many capable people from serving on boards, simply because they did not want to be bothered getting certified.

- I am not sure that directors as a class have much impact on society.

- I believe very strongly that qualified directors can make a significant contribution—a difference—to the performance of a public company, which translates into value to the shareholders, investors, the economy and, by extension, society. This more than justifies the pains and tribulations involved in earning the accreditation.

Past and Current Boards of the Author (1963 to 2002)

FOR-PROFIT BOARDS

a)   Unrelated to Employment

1.   American Eco Corporation
2.   Canada Development Corporation
3.   Canadian Business Media Limited *
4.   Camreal Corporation
5.   Canron Limited (*formerly Canada Iron Limited*)
6.   Capstone Investments Limited
7.   CBOC Continental Limited (*formerly Continental Bank of Canada*)
8.   Coscan Limited (*formerly Costain Limited*)

---

* Board Chairman

9. Enbridge Corporation *(formerly IPL Energy Inc and, prior to that, Interhome Limited and prior to that, Interprovincial Pipelines Limited)*
10. e-tech direct *(Advisory Board)*
11. Florentine Shops Limited
12. Home Capital Group Incorporated*
13. Home Oil Company Limited
14. Home Trust Company *(formerly Home Savings and Loan Corporation)*
15. Interlink Freight Systems Limited *(formerly CP Express and Transport Limited)**
16. Interprovincial Pipelines Limited
17. Interprovincial Pipelines (NW) Limited
18. Magellan Aerospace Corporation *(formerly Fleet Aerosopace Corporation*)*
19. Malibu Engineering & Software Limited *
20. Minacs Worldwide Inc.
21. Monsanto Canada Limited*
22. Monsanto Canada Growth and Innovation Council *(Advisory Board)*
23. Perigee Inc.*
24. Polysar Chemical Company*
25. Primaris Corporate Services Limited*
26. Royal LePage Commercial Advisory Board*
27. Sears Acceptance Company
28. Sears Canada Limited
29. Silcorp Limited
30. Swiss Re Holdings Limited*
31. Swiss Re Canada Life and Health Canada Limited* *(formerly Swiss Reassurance Company of Canada*)*
32. Swiss Reinsurance Company Canada*
33. The General Accident Insurance Company of Canada

* Board Chairman

b)   Related to Employment

1. A.E. LePage Limited
2. Canlea Development Limited
3. Comac Communications Limited
4. Delta Hotels Limited
5. Harlequin Enterprises Limited
6. London Insurance Group Limited
7. London Life Insurance Company
8. Metrospan Newspapers Limited
9. Neilsen-Ferns Limited
10. Newsweb Limited*
11. Royal LePage Limited
12. Toronto Star Newspapers Limited
13. Torstar Corporation
14. Trilon Financial Corporation
15. Trizec Corporation
16. Union Carbide Canada Limited
17. Visking Limited

---

* Board Chairman

(The author has also sat on forty not-for-profit boards, task forces, and equivalent bodies.)

INDEX

Accountability, 19, 51
Accountability chain, 52
Accreditation. *See* Public
    company director accreditation
Advisory boards, 57–68
    advantages/disadvantages, 57–58,
      63
    case histories, 65–68
    prevalence, 59
    private companies, 60–61, 64
    public companies, 60, 64
    uses, 61–63
Alcan Aluminum, 104
Amelio, Gilbert E., 126
Annoying traits, 23–25
Annual retainer, 107
Astley, Bob, 98
Atkinson, Joe, 46
Author, 44–47, 95–100
    CEO succession, 78–79
    company/board ceased to
      function, 199–203
    conflicts of interest, 95–96
    corporate insolvency, 155–159
    list of past/present boards,
      229–231
    Perigee, 98–99
    Primaris, 96–97
    Trizec, 34–35

Bank of Montreal, 28
Basic principles, 5–7, 205–211
Bausch & Lomb, 104
Benedict, Ben, 46
Berkshire Hathaway, 104
Black, Fischer, 139

Black-Scholes option pricing
    model, 139–140
Blair, Bob, 201–202
Board book, 17
Board chairman. *See* CEO/chairman
Board committees, 12–13, 16
Board manners, 23–25
Board of directors
    CCAA, 159
    compensation. *See* Director
      compensation
    conflicts of interest, 35–36
    delegation, 30–32
    frequency of meeting, 16
    liability, 194–197
    number of directors, 12
    pension fund management,
      86–94
    replacement of directors, 19
    retirement age, 19, 28, 41–42,
      84–86
    self-assessment, 18, 51–56
    structure, 12–20
    time requirements, 111–112
Bonus, 114
Brascan, 96
Bre-X, 216
Brooks, Mel, 20
Buffet, Warren, 39, 104, 142, 167
Bush, George W., 171

Cadbury Report, 114
Campbell, Bill, 46
Canada Development Corporation,
    201–202
Canadian Business Media Limited,

200
Canadian Pacific, 156
Canadian parliamentary system, 192
Canadian-U.S. differences
  CEO/chairman, roles, 191
  constraints on management freedom, 193
  director compensation, 104–105, 110–111
  government, 192
  ownership structure, 192
  share price performance, 193–194
Capitalism for Tomorrow (Sykes/ Serjeants), 173
Carson, Dick, 4
Carson, Johnny, 27
Cash retainer fees, 114
CCAA, 159
CEO/chairman
  responsibilities, 14–15, 41
  separation of roles, 33, 69–73, 191
  succession. *See* CEO succession
CEO succession, 30–31, 74–84
  author's experience, 78–79
  controlling shareholder, 77–78
  ideal scenario, 81–84
  wholly-owned companies, 31, 74–76
  widely held company, 80–81
Charitable donations, 171–172
Chief executive officer. *See* CEO/chairman
Churchill, Winston, 213
Cisco Systems, 104
Co-stakeholder model, 173
Compensation, 103–115
  annual retainer, 107
  Canadian-U.S. differences, 104–105, 110–111
  compensation mix, 113
  criticism, 103
  how much to pay, 109–113
  meeting fee, 107–108
  setting the compensation, 108–109
  share ownership, 105–106
  stock grants, 38, 106, 114, 115

stock options. *See* Stock options
  time requirements, 111–112
Conflicts of interest, 35–36, 96
Constituency boards, 13–14, 41
Constructive interaction, 6n
Continuing education, 30
Core principles, 5–7, 205–211
Corporate insolvency, 155–159
Corporate responsibility, 163–174
  charitable donations, 171–172
  conference (1996), 168
  Delaware, 163–164, 166
  downsizing, 168–169
  shareholders, 167–168, 170–172, 174
  stakeholders, 165–168, 172–174
Costain, 95, 96
Coté, Pierre, 201
Couche-Tard, 158
Creative tension, 6
Crystal, Graef, 104, 125, 144
Current status of corporate governance, 211–213

Deferred stock units, 114n
Delaware, 163–164, 166
Delegation, 30–32
Dewar, Jack, 45
Dimma, William. *See* Author
Director accreditation. *See* Public company director accreditation
Director retirement, 19, 28, 41–42, 84–86
Dodge v. Ford Motor Company, 164
Downsizing, 168–169
Due diligence defence, 194–197
Dunlop, Chainsaw Al, 171

Eisner, Michael, 129
Executive committee, 13
Executive compensation, 123–153
  criticism, 123–124
  miscellaneous facts, 124–127
  pensions, 145–153
  performance, and, 130–131
  self-correcting levels, 134
  societal implications, 132–133
  stock options, 134–145. *See also* Stock options
  upward bias, 131–132

Executive pensions, 145–153

Florentine Shop, 4
Frank Russell, 89
Friedman, Milton, 172

Galbraith, J.K., 133
Gender-neutral language, 6n
General Accident Assurance, 95, 96
Gordon, Walter, 45
Gray, Gordon, 95
Greenwald, Gerald, 168

Hall, Brian, 125
Hampson, Tony, 202
Hanks, James, 164
Hayden, Salter, 46
Hills Stores, 189
Hindmarsh, Ruth, 46
Hostile takeover, 187–190, 201

Ideal processes, 14–20
Ideal structure, 12–14
Individual director assessment, 19,
    27–28, 54–56
Insolvency, 155–159
Institutional investors, 175–185
    management self-interest vs.
        shareholder interests, 176–178
    mutual funds, 182
    pension funds, 180–181, 184–185
    shareholder influence, 182–183
Interlink Freight Systems, 155–157,
    200
Isautier, Bernard, 202

Jordon, Michael, 129

Karmazin, Mel, 124
Keynes, John Maynard, 89

Lambert, Allen, 46, 85
Lead director, 40–41
Legg Mason, 99
Letterman, David, 27
Leveraged stock purchase programs,
    135
Liability, 194–197
Loewen, Ray, 188
Loewen Group, 188

London Life, 96
Lorsch, Jay, 55
Lynch, Peter, 158

Madonna, 129
Making Boards Work
    (Leighton/Thain), 4
Management self-interest vs.
    shareholder interests, 176–178
Mandatory share ownership
    requirements, 105
Meeting fee, 107–108
Microsoft, 142
Modified tontine approach, 108
Monsanto Canada, 65–66, 200
Moore Corporation, 190
Mushroom theory, 94
Mutual funds, 182
Myth and Reality (Mace), 4

Nellcor, 189
New Corporate Directors, The
    (Anderson/Anthony), 4
Nininger, Jim, 2

Ontario Teachers' Plan, 181
Option repricing, 140–141
Options. See Stock options
Overarching premises, 5–7, 205–211

Paramount, 188
Pawns and Potentates (Lorsch), 4
Pension funds, 180–181, 184–185
Pensions
    executive, 145–153
    management of, as board
        function, 86–94
Perfect board, 11–21
Perigee, 98–99
Personal experiences. See Author
Political correctness, 13
Polysar Chemical Company,
    202–203
Primaris Corporate Services, 96–97
Profit maximization, 171
Public company director
    accreditation, 117–121, 215–227
    mandatory vs. voluntary
        accreditation, 221–222
    objections, 119–120, 219–221

other people's comments,
224–227
process of, 217–219
Puritan-Bennett, 189

Questionnaire, 53

Registered pension plan (RPP), 148,
153
Reprehensible traits, 23–25
Retirement age, 19, 28, 41–42,
84–86
Ridout, Derek, 158
Rogers Communications, 200
Royal LePage, 65, 95
RPP, 148, 153
Rubin, Robert, 137–138

Scholes, Myron, 139
Schremp, Jürgen, 189
SEI, 89
Self-assessment, 18, 51–56
Senior executive compensation.
    See Executive compensation
Separation of roles, 33, 69–73, 191
Serjeants, Graham, 173
SERPs, 146–153
Service Corp. International, 188
Shakespeare, William, 47
Shareholder capitalism, 170–172,
174
Shareholder influence, 182–183
Shareholder rights plan, 178, 183
Shareholder value, 189
Shareholders, 167–168
Silcorp Limited, 157–158
Sinclair, Ian, 46
Smaller companies, 29
Speaking out, 34
Stakeholder capitalism, 172–174
Stakeholder statutes, 165
Stakeholder theory, 165, 168
Statutory liabilities, 194–197
Stock grants, 38, 106, 114, 115, 135
Stock options, 32, 38–39, 134–145
    accounting treatment, 141–142
    Black-Scholes model, 139–140
    criticism, 106
    executives, for, 134–138
    ground rules, 106–107
    option repricing, 140–141

performance options, 136–137,
143–144
when granted, 114–115
Strategic plan, 15–16
Subsidiary CEO succession, 31. See
also CEO succession
Succession. See CEO succession
Sun Microsystems, 104
Supplemental executive retirement
plans (SERPs), 146–153
Sykes, Allen, 173

Takeover bid, 178–179, 187–190,
201–203
Thain, Don, 118
Thermo-Electron, 189
Time requirements, 111–112
Time Warner, 188
Time Warner case, 166–167
Tontine, 108n
Toronto Star Newspapers, 46
Torstar Corporation, 46
Total shareholder return (TSR), 179
Training, 30
Trizec Corporation, 34, 96
TSR, 179

U.S.-Canadian differences. See
Canadian-U.S. differences
U.S. directors, 39–40
Underperforming directors, 56
Union Carbide Canada, 45–46

Vanilla plan, 178, 183
Volkswagen, 189

Wallace Computer Services, 190
War stories. See Author
Welch, Jack, 127, 129
Who's in Charge Here, Anyway?
(Zimmerman), 4
Wholly-owned subsidiaries
    CEO succession, 31, 74–76
    separation of roles
    (CEO/chairman), 70
Widely held companies
    CEO succession, 80–81
    separation of roles
    (CEO/chairman), 71
Wilson, Alex, 98